# CONTENTS

**028**
## SADDAM HUSSEIN
The butcher of Baghdad

**038**
## TORNADO GR.1
The versatile and long-serving RAF jet made its debut during Desert Storm

**034**
## OPERATION DESERT SHIELD
Ensuring the safety of Saudi Arabia and preparing the offensive against Iraq

# 062
# OPERATION DESERT STORM
One of the most successful campaigns of the 20th century

# 022

# 068

# 122

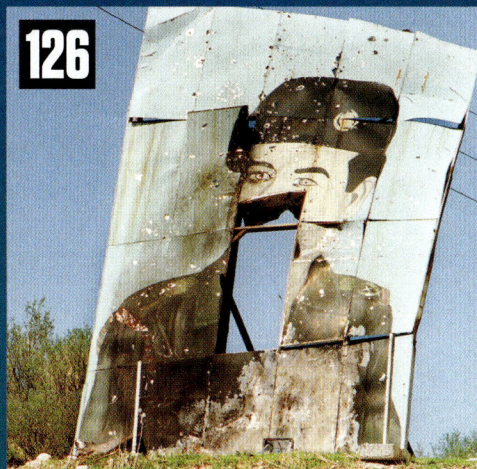

# 126

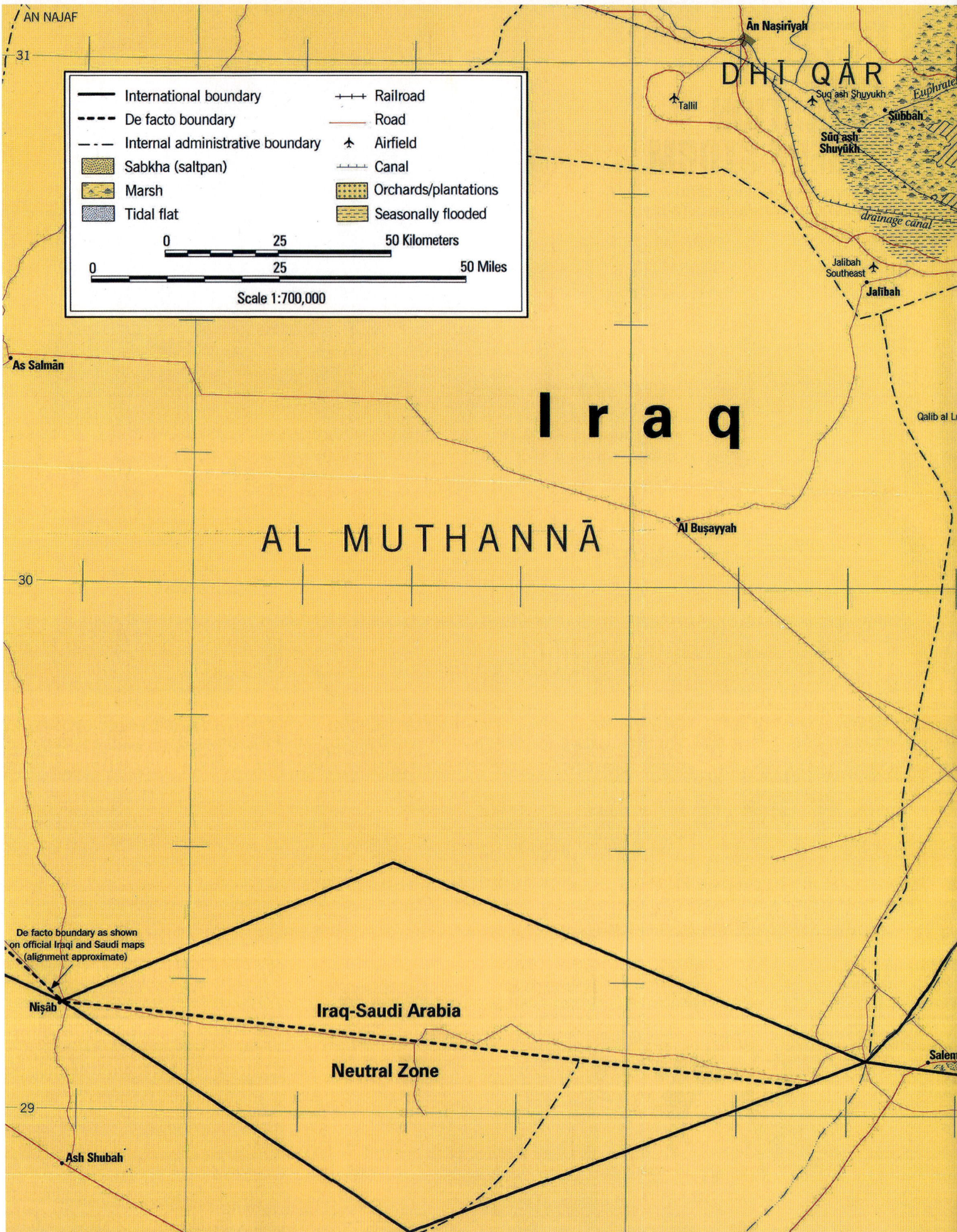

AN NAJAF

31

Ān Naṣirīyah

DHĪ QĀR

Tallil

Suq ash Shuyukh

Euphrate

Ṣubbah

Sūq ash
Shuyūkh

drainage canal

Jalibah
Southeast

Jalībah

**Legend:**

- International boundary
- De facto boundary
- Internal administrative boundary
- Sabkha (saltpan)
- Marsh
- Tidal flat
- Railroad
- Road
- ✈ Airfield
- Canal
- Orchards/plantations
- Seasonally flooded

0   25   50 Kilometers

0   25   50 Miles

Scale 1:700,000

As Salmān

**I r a q**

Qalib al L

**AL MUTHANNĀ**

Al Buṣayyah

30

De facto boundary as shown
on official Iraqi and Saudi maps
(alignment approximate)

Niṣāb

**Iraq-Saudi Arabia**

Salem

**Neutral Zone**

29

Ash Shubah

Al Qurnah
Al Muzayri'ah
Al Kaba'ish
ud
Ash Shanin
Dowa
Al Madinah
Qurna

Hawr al Hammār
(marsh)

An Nashwah
Shahbān

Iran

KHUZESTĀN

Hamrīnān
Al Wākī
Ar Rumaylah
Al Ma'qil

AL BASRAH

Imān Ānas
Basrah Maqal
Al Başrah
Basrah West
Shaibah
Az Zubayr
Shaibah West
Ar Rumaylah Southwest
Az Zubayr

Khorramshahr
Abū al Khaşīb
Abadan Intl
Abādān

Bandar-e Khomeynī

Rūd-e
Kārūn

Al Mufrash

Khawr az Zubayr

seasonally flooded

Khosrowābād

Safwan
Safwān
'Abdalī
Umm Qaşr

Nahr-e Qaşr
Al Fāw

Warbah

Ar Rawdatayn

Būbiyān

Khawr 'Abd Allāh

Kuwait

Qaşr as Sabīyah

Maskān
Faylakah
Kuwait Bay
Az Zawr
'Awhah

Al Jahrah
Ad Dawhah (Doha)
KUWAIT
ferry
Abraq
Ali al Salem
As Sālimīyah
Hawalli
Abraq Khītan
Al Funaytis
Al Farwānīyah
Kuwait Intl.

Persian Gulf

Al Maqwā

25 meters

Al Ahmadi
Al Fuḥayḥīl
Mīnā' al Ahmadi
Kubbar
Ahmadi
Ash Shu'aybah
Mīnā' 'Abd Allāh

Ahmed al Jaber

Ra's al Qulay'ah

Former boundary of Kuwait-Saudi Arabia Neutral Zone

Qārūh

# A TIMELINE OF THE GULF WAR

The first conflict of the 1990s saw a huge United Nations coalition liberate Kuwait from Iraqi occupation in the largest military alliance assembled since WWII

**2-4 August 1990**

**2 August 1990**

**2 August 1990**

*Saddam Hussein prays in the Kuwaiti desert after Iraq's invasion of the country*

### INVASION OF KUWAIT

Under the leadership of Saddam Hussein, Iraqi forces invade Kuwait to gain more control over its oil supply. Kuwaiti forces are overwhelmed and Saudi Arabia comes under the threat of invasion. A follow-up conquest of Saudi Arabia has the potential to leave 40 percent of the world's oil reserves under Saddam's dictatorial control.

### BATTLE OF DASMAN PALACE 01

Jaber Al-Ahmad Al-Sabah, Emir of Kuwait, is forced to leave his residence at Dasman Palace when it is attacked by Iraqi Special Forces and elements of the Iraqi Republican Guard. The emir vacates the premises in a helicopter to Saudi Arabia but his younger brother, Sheikh Fahd Al-Ahmad is killed.

### BRITISH AIRWAYS FLIGHT 149 02

385 passengers and crew of a BA flight are captured by Iraqi forces after landing at Kuwait International Airport. A diplomatic crisis develops when the passengers and crew are held as hostages with some being used as 'human shields' to deter UN military operations. One Kuwaiti passenger is killed while the rest of the hostages are released after negotiations with Saddam Hussein are undertaken by the former British Prime Minister Edward Heath.

*The BA Boeing 747-116 aircraft is destroyed by Iraqi forces*

American and Saudi Arabian fighter jets fly over burning oil wells over Kuwait, 17 January 1991

## NAVAL OPERATIONS

The Iraqi Navy is almost completely destroyed in the Persian Gulf by Coalition naval forces. After a series of engagements at Ad-Dawrah, Qurah, Maradim and Bubiyan, the Iraqis lose over 100 vessels of all types, including 19 sunken ships.

USS Missouri fires its 16-inch guns as night shelling of Iraqi targets takes place along the northern Kuwaiti coast

Source: Wiki / PD Gov

The remains of one of the two American F-16 aircraft that are shot down during the airstrike. Their pilots are captured by Iraqi forces

Source: Wiki / PD Gov

## PACKAGE Q STRIKE 03

The largest airstrike of the war occurs when the US Air Force attacks a number of targets in Baghdad. The main target is Tuwaitha Nuclear Research Centre but American aircraft fail to destroy it. Seventy-eight American aircraft take part, including 56 F-16 Fighting Falcons.

## OPERATION DESERT STORM

Desert Storm begins when the Coalition flies over 100,000 sorties and drops almost 90,000 tons of bombs against Iraqi positions in Iraq and Kuwait. The Coalition quickly gains air superiority over the numerically inferior Iraqi Air Force and their success enables Desert Storm's ground offensive to commence.

**17 January-23 February 1991**

**29 November 1990**

**18 January-2 February 1991**

**19 January 1991**

**29 January-1 February 1991**

## THE COALITION FORMS

UN Security Council Resolution 678 orders Iraq to withdraw from Kuwait by 15 January 1991. In the event of Iraq's non-compliance with the resolution, a UN coalition forms to liberate Kuwait by force. It is led by the US but comprises 35 other countries including Saudi Arabia, Britain, Egypt and France.

*The United Nations Security Council votes to authorise the use of military force against Iraq in New York*

© Getty

## BATTLE OF KHAFJI 04

The first major ground engagement of the war takes place in and around the Saudi Arabian city of Khafji after Saddam Hussein orders an invasion of the country. Three Iraqi divisions invade and briefly occupy Khafji before Saudi-led Coalition forces recapture the city.

*Qatari tank soldiers celebrate at Khafji, February 1991*

© Alamy

PACKAGE Q STRIKE **03**

BATTLE OF 73 EASTING **05**

BATTLE OF RUMAILA **08**

BATTLE OF NORFOLK **06**

BATTLE OF KUWAIT INTERNATIONAL AIRPORT **07**

BRITISH AIRWAYS FLIGHT 149 **02**

BATTLE OF DASMAN PALACE **01**

BATTLE OF KHAFJI **04**

## "OVER 2,000 VEHICLES ARE DESTROYED ALONG THE HIGHWAY ALONG WITH THOUSANDS OF IRAQI CASUALTIES"

**24-28 February 1991**

**25-27 February 1991**

**26-27 February 1991**

# LIBERATION OF KUWAIT

American-led Coalition forces launch the ground offensive of Operation Desert Storm to liberate Kuwait. The Iraqis withdraw from the country and most of the fighting occurs in Iraq itself. The liberation only takes four days to achieve after almost seven months of Iraqi occupation.

*An F-14 flies over a burning oil field in Kuwait*

# HIGHWAY OF DEATH

American, British, Canadian and French aircraft attack retreating Iraqi vehicles and personnel along Highway 80 – a six-lane road that runs from Kuwait City into Iraq towards Basra. Over 2,000 vehicles are destroyed along the highway along with thousands of Iraqi casualties, the majority of whom are captured.

*Abandoned vehicles and equipment litter the road out of Kuwait into Iraq*

# BATTLE OF 73 EASTING **05**

Several Iraqi armoured divisions are decisively defeated by American and British forces in a grid coordinate area known as '73 Easting'. The Iraqis lose 160 tanks, 200 other vehicles and approximately 2,300 casualties. The Coalition only suffers losses of six killed, 19 wounded and one tracked vehicle.

## BATTLE OF RUMAILA 08

The last battle of the war occurs after the ceasefire when the US 24th Infantry Division engages a withdrawing force of Iraqi armoured forces. The battle begins when Iraqi soldiers fire on an American patrol that enters their path of retreat. Over 700 Iraqi troops are killed, 3,000 are captured and hundreds of armoured vehicles are destroyed. There are no American fatalities.

*A destroyed Iraqi column of vehicles, including a T-72 tank on Highway 8, pictured two days after the Battle of Rumaila*

*Source: Wiki / PD.gov*

*The debris remains of a transport aircraft and a small jet after the Coalition bomb Kuwait International Airport*

*Source: Wiki / PD*

## BATTLE OF KUWAIT INTERNATIONAL AIRPORT 07

Combined elements of 18 American and Iraqi divisions fight for control of Kuwait City's airport. The US 1st and 2nd Marine Divisions also enter the city and encounter fierce resistance. Other major pieces of the city's infrastructure, as well as the nearby airport, are destroyed or severely damaged. A major tank battle occurs at the airport with the Americans winning the battle.

*© Getty*

**27 February 1991**

**27 February 1991**

**2 March 1991**

**28 February 1991**

## BATTLE OF NORFOLK 06

Named after 'Objective Norfolk' – an intersection of roads, desert trails and an Iraqi supply depot – this battle is a huge tank engagement between American, British and Iraqi armoured forces. Approximately 850 Iraqi tanks, along with hundreds of other combat vehicles, are destroyed in the second largest tank battle in American history after the Battle of the Bulge.

*A silhouette of two Challenger tanks and their crews. British Challengers perform particularly well at Norfolk where none are lost to enemy action*

*Source: Wiki / UK Ministry of Defence*

## CEASEFIRE

US President George H. W. Bush announces a ceasefire in hostilities after the liberation of Kuwait City. Bush succinctly states, "Kuwait is liberated. Iraq's army is defeated. Our military objectives are met."

*A member of the Kuwaiti resistance raises his rifle and national flag after the announcement of the ceasefire*

*© Getty*

# THE LIONS OF MESOPOTAMIA

Born in the ashes of war, the nation of Iraq was destined to play a defining role in the Middle East throughout the 20th century, a period marked by brutal conflict and clashing geopolitical interests

**WORDS: CHARLES GINGER**

Hussein's hand trembled as he stared at the letter. Could this really be happening? Could his dream of a united Arab nation finally be looming over the horizon into view? The British certainly seemed to think so, if Sir Henry McMahon's correspondence was accurate. In return for Hussein triggering an uprising against the Ottomans, who were locked in the death struggle of the Great War against the British and its empire, McMahon, in his capacity as the High Commissioner of Egypt, was promising British support for the creation of an Arab state that would stretch from Aleppo to Aden. And who better to lead this new nation than Hussein, Sharif of Mecca and son of the House of Hashim? The royal family of Jordan had held sway over the holy city since the 10th century, and if they could drive the Ottomans out, the Hashemites would control the Arabian Peninsula, Greater Syria and the rocky lands of Iraq. The time of the Turks was over. The dawn of Arab dominion was at hand.

*Images: Getty Images, Alamy*

Faisal al-Hussein, better known as King Faisal I, accedes to the throne of the Kingdom of Iraq

# THE RISE AND FALL OF IRAQ

*Defining moment*
## END OF BRITISH MANDATE
## 1932

In the wake of a devastating revolt triggered by years of British interference in Iraqi matters, the Kingdom of Iraq is finally granted full independence. Iraqi control over its own destiny is brought about via the Anglo-Iraqi Treaty signed two years before by High Commissioner Francis Humphrys and Iraqi Prime Minister Nuri al-Said. Unfortunately, the country will be shaken by a spate of coups before a move to align with Hitler's Germany proves a step too far for the British.

**BRITISH SEIZE BAGHDAD**
After seeing an entire army destroyed in the siege of Kut Al Amara in 1915, the British recover to strike a fatal blow to Ottoman hopes of victory by taking the Iraqi capital.
*1917*

**KING FAISAL I CROWNED**
While independence was still over a decade away, the coronation of Faisal as king was a key step towards a sovereign Iraq, although the British decision to appoint a Sunni monarch in a Shia-dominated realm would in time create division.
*1921*

**BRITAIN RE-OCCUPIES IRAQ**
Determined to halt a potential Axis encroachment on its Middle Eastern interests, Britain uses the terms of the Anglo-Iraqi Treaty to justify an invasion.
*1941*

**JOINING THE ARAB LEAGUE**
Egypt, Syria, Transjordan, Iraq, Saudi Arabia and Lebanon comprise the six founding members of the Arab League, a network established in Cairo with a view to enhancing collaboration between the Arab states.
*1945*

*In the wake of the First World War the region was split along lines decided by the British and French governments after the fall of the Ottoman Empire*

### Defining moment
## 14 JULY REVOLUTION
### 1958

Years of bubbling tensions finally boil over as General Qasim launches a ruthless coup in which the royal family is marched out into the courtyard of the al-Rahab Palace and shot. King Faisal suffers grievous wounds to the head and neck and is bundled into a car. He soon bleeds to death. The Hashemite Kingdom of Iraq dies with him. Qasim becomes Prime Minister and Minister of Defence, while his co-conspirator Abdul Salam Arif is appointed as Qasim's deputy, as well as Minister of the Interior.

### Defining moment
## SADDAM BECOMES PRESIDENT
### 1979

In a watershed moment for Iraq and the wider world, Saddam Hussein Abd al-Majid al-Tikriti, still in his early 40s, replaces his ill cousin Ahmed al-Bakr as President. While he will oversee progress in various areas, including an expansion of the economy and religious freedom for minorities he wishes to bring on side, his rule will be shaped by violence and oppression, including costly invasions of Iran and Kuwait, the slaughter of thousands of innocent citizens and other human rights offences. A dictator in all but name, his grip on Iraq will remain vice-like for over two decades.

**KURDISTAN DEMOCRATIC PARTY FOUNDED**
With Soviet backing, the KDP is created in Iranian Kurdistan. Mustafa Barzani, a tribal leader, is chosen as commander of the Kurdish Army with a view to spearheading the revolution against Iraq.
*1946*

**KUWAIT GAINS INDEPENDENCE**
Having agreed with the British to nullify the terms of the Anglo-Kuwaiti Treaty of 1899, on 19 June 1961 Kuwait becomes a fully independent state. Benefitting from huge oil reserves, it is a wealthy nation, one coveted by Iraq.
*1961*

**Ba'athists snatch power**
Unwilling to abandon their dreams of power, the Ba'athists finally gain a stranglehold after a bloodless coup removes Arif's son. Their triumph is thanks in no small part to Saddam Hussein's efforts to reorganise a once divided party.
*1968*

**PETROL COMPANY NATIONALISED**
After years of failed negotiations and rising tensions between the oil companies operating in Iraq and the government, the Iraq Petroleum Company is nationalised.
*1972*

**WAR WITH IRAN BEGINS**
A disastrous war that will kill between 1 and 2 million people and ultimately end in a stalemate is triggered by Iraq suddenly invading its neighbour Iran, beginning with a largely unsuccessful series of airstrikes using Soviet-made aircraft.
*1980*

# CARVING OUT A KINGDOM

## If the people of Iraq wanted full autonomy, they were going to have to fight for it

The deserts, mountains and marshes that comprise the nation of Iraq may be ancient, but the country itself is little over a century old. Even so, the roots of its diverse peoples reach back far beyond the birth of the Kingdom of Iraq in 1921, and as with almost every new dynasty, the road to King Faisal's coronation was strewn with shattered dreams and broken bodies.

After allying itself with Germany and Austria-Hungary in the early stages of WWI, the Ottoman Empire found itself embroiled in direct conflict with the Allies, chiefly Britain and her colonies. The Mesopotamian Campaign began in November 1914 with the British capture of Basra and its surrounding oilfields. It would conclude on 30 October 1918 with the signing of the Armistice of Mudros (an island located in the Aegean Sea), a treaty that spelled the beginning of the end for the Ottomans. However, it wasn't just the tenacity of the British military that did for an empire founded in 1299 that spanned from the shores of the Adriatic to the Persian Gulf. The Ottomans' greatest enemy was not beyond its borders – it was inside them.

Convinced by his son Abdullah to eschew dreams of ruling part of Arabia within the overall confines of Ottoman hegemony in favour of striving for command of a totally sovereign Arab state, Hussein bin Ali launched the Arab Revolt on 10 June 1916. Aided by the British, who in October dispatched a young captain by the name of TE Lawrence to Hejaz (a region that comprises vast swathes of Saudi Arabia's western coast) to lend his expertise, the Sharifian Army (named in honour of Sharif Hussein) waged a long, bloody but ultimately successful campaign against their Ottoman overlords. Working alongside the likes of Lawrence of Arabia, the Sharifians sabotaged Ottoman supply lines, blew up railways and pinned the enemy down in exhausting battles that diverted men and materiel away from the front lines.

Baghdad fell in March 1917, and on 1 October 1918 Arab cavalry rode triumphantly into Damascus. Ottoman dreams of victory were in tatters, and further humiliation followed in November when the British, tired of the Ottomans continuing to insist on their right to retain parts of Iraq, occupied Constantinople. The way was now clear for the foundations of a new nation to be laid, just as Hussein and his sons (including Faisal, who commanded the Northern Army during the revolt and tried to broker a private deal with the Ottomans that would have given him his own kingdom) always hoped. However, the British proved to be duplicitous allies.

Having secretly agreed to the terms of the Sykes-Picot Agreement in 1916 (a plan

*King Faisal I attends a peace conference in Paris in 1919. To his far left stands Nuri al-said, and to his immediate right is TE Lawrence, better known as Lawrence of Arabia*

*Victorious British troops march captured Ottoman soldiers through the streets of Baghdad. March 1917*

finalised by British diplomat Mark Sykes and his French counterpart Francois Georges-Picot), in 1918 Britain was readying to cement its hold on Palestine, Jordan and southern Iraq, along with the ports of Haifa and Acre. The French were preparing to do likewise in Syria, Lebanon, southern Turkey and the Kurdistan Region of Iraq. As part of this treacherous agreement, Britain was granted a Mandate for Mesopotamia by the League of Nations in 1920.

Rightly outraged at their erstwhile allies reneging on the deal struck between McMahon and Hussein and fearful their country was about to be swallowed by the British Empire, the Iraqis rose up. Resentment spread through religious groups and tribes, spilling out into protests in May 1920. When their peaceful efforts bore no fruit, the people of Iraq took up arms, urged on by the Shia leader Ayatollah Muhammad Taqi al-Shirazi, who called on his fellow countrymen to demand their rights: "In demanding them they should maintain peace and order. But if the English prevent them from obtaining their rights it is permitted to make use of defensive force."

The ensuing violence lasted for months and claimed the lives of thousands. The hated British mandate also perished in the bloodied streets of Iraq, lingering on only in spirit until 1932, when, as agreed by the delegates at a conference held in Cairo in 1921, Iraq was granted full independence. By then it had been ruled by Faisal for 11 years.

King Faisal I's reign witnessed Iraq joining the League of Nations and the furtherance of its claim over Kuwait. According to the Iraqi Government, prior to its seizure by the British, jurisdiction over Kuwait resided with the former Ottoman vilayet (province) of Basra. Therefore, Kuwait was little more than a British invention, meaning the territory was rightfully Iraq's, a claim that would have dire consequences for the region decades later.

Faisal's rule was ended in September 1933 by a fatal heart attack during a trip to Switzerland. He left behind a nation riddled with tensions, with many of his former subjects chafing at the ongoing presence of the British, who continued to operate military bases in Iraq and retained the right to move troops around the country in accordance with the Anglo-Iraqi Treaty of 1930. While some politicians, such as Nuri al-Said, accepted British influence, others, like Rashid Ali al-Gaylani, who would serve as Prime Minister on three occasions, were fervent believers in Arab nationalism and wanted the imperialists gone.

Faisal's son, Ghazi, inherited a divided kingdom beset by lethally ambitious figures. Arguably the worst among them was the brutal Kurdish general Bakr Sidqi. A veteran of the Balkan Wars of 1912–13, Sidqi served in British intelligence before rising through the ranks of the Iraqi military.

In August 1933, he oversaw the Simele massacre, in which 3,000 supposed Assyrian separatists were slaughtered by the Royal Iraqi Army. He would later deal with a spate of Shia tribal rebellions with equal ferocity and launch his own coup in 1936, which succeeded in replacing Prime Minister Yasin al-Hashimi with a Sidqi ally. However, the mastermind of the first military coup in the modern Arab world didn't get to enjoy the benefits of placing friends in high places for long. In 1937, Sidqi was assassinated in the garden of an air base in Mosul.

Ever plagued by murder and misfortune, Iraq endured several upheavals throughout King Ghazi's short reign, with coups, uprisings and assassinations constantly shifting the political landscape. The beleaguered country then lost its monarch on 4 April 1939 when Ghazi died in a car accident. Many in Iraq suspected that the British had colluded with Nuri al-Said to cause the crash due to Ghazi's hopes of unifying Kuwait and Iraq.

Like his father before him, Ghazi only sired one son, a boy named Faisal. The child would succeed him at just three years old, with his father's cousin Prince 'Abd al-Ilah serving as regent until Faisal was old enough to rule as king. He would be Iraq's last.

# LAND GRAB: THE STRUGGLE FOR KUWAIT

Oil was for many years a blessing and a curse for Kuwait. Craved by the wider world, who were only too willing to pay handsome fees, the black oceans beneath its soil propelled Kuwait to incredible wealth, an influx of hundreds of millions that drew envious gazes, especially from Iraq. Pointing to the fact that the League of Nations designated Kuwait as part of the province of Basra, a province the Ottomans refused to relinquish, many Iraqis consistently called for it to be absorbed into Iraq, labelling Kuwait as a British creation. For their part, the Kuwaitis argued that the 1899 agreement between Shaykh Mubarak Al Sabah and the British, which enabled Kuwait to establish its own international agreements with other nations, proved beyond all doubt that it was a fully independent country well before the idea of an Iraqi state was even considered. While there was once a time when union with Iraq was a popular notion, by the 1960s Kuwait was raking in vast oil revenues, greatly diminishing calls to surrender its sovereignty.

*Kuwait is home to approximately eight per cent of the world's oil reserves, while Iraq boasts almost 12 per cent*

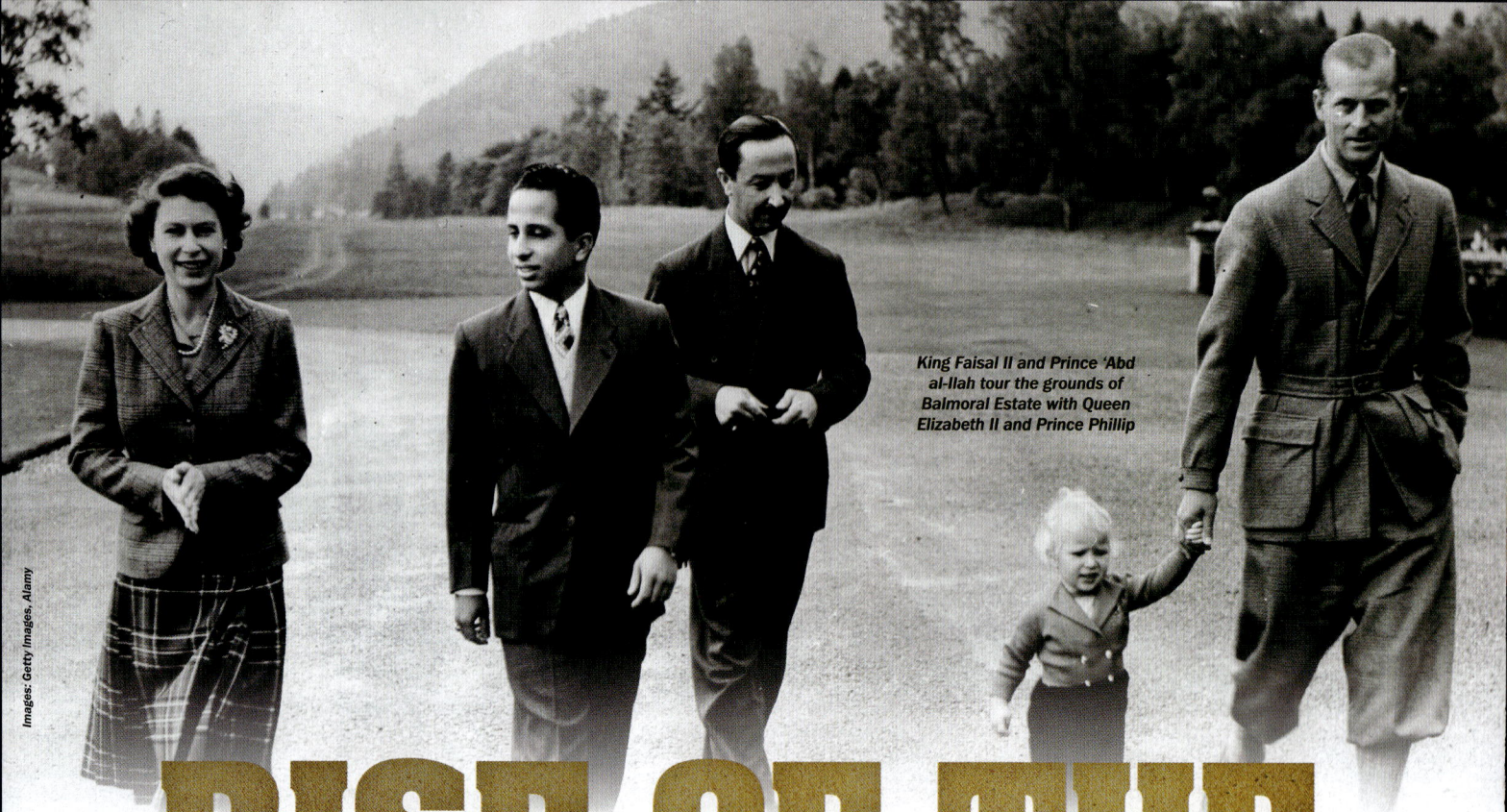

King Faisal II and Prince 'Abd al-Ilah tour the grounds of Balmoral Estate with Queen Elizabeth II and Prince Phillip

# RISE OF THE REPUBLIC

## Haunted by zealous military figures determined to overthrow the established order, Iraq's monarchy stood no chance

Young Faisal was still shy of his sixth birthday when pro-German Prime Minister al-Gaylani launched a coup in Baghdad on 3 April 1941 as WWII raged. Believing the Third Reich supported the Arab cause, al-Gaylani, who hailed from Sunni aristocracy, snatched power from Prince al-Ilah. Not about to allow the Axis powers to gain a foothold in the Middle East, Britain promptly occupied Iraq, forcing al-Gaylani to flee to Berlin. Spirited away to England when al-Gaylani lunged for power, Faisal attended Harrow School in London, where he studied alongside his cousin Hussein, the future king of Jordan. He returned home when the dust settled, and in May 1953 he assumed the throne as a ruler in his own right.

Determined to modernise Iraq, Faisal used soaring oil profits to construct dams, bridges, schools and hospitals. Perhaps in time Faisal's grand plans may have come to fruition, but his interests were not only domestic. In February 1955, Faisal signed up to the Baghdad Pact (formerly known as the Central Treaty Organization, or CENTO), an anti-Soviet alliance with Britain, Pakistan, Turkey and Iran.

The Arab nationalists were enraged at Faisal's decision to strengthen ties with Britain. Fearful of the influence of the United Arab Republic (a political union of Syria and Egypt), Faisal countered with his own federation by uniting Iraq and Jordan. Neither survived for long.

Sharing the hatred many Iraqis held towards the pro-Western policies of the monarchy, 'Abd al-Karim Qasim longed for change. As the gulf between the elites loyal to King Faisal and the disgruntled working classes yawned ever wider in the summer of 1958, Qasim, a colonel in the Iraqi military, capitalised on pre-arranged troop movements to stage the bloody overthrow of Faisal and his retinue. Marching his troops to the capital, he forced the king from power in the 14 July Revolution.

In a bid to avert bloodshed, Faisal selflessly ordered his royal guard to surrender. He was promptly marched outside into the courtyard of his palace and shot alongside Prince al-Ilah and other members of the monarchy. Faisal's corpse was strung up, while al-Ilah's body was "dragged into the street like that of a dog and torn limb from limb".

Proclaiming the birth of a republic, Qasim set about attempting to unify Iraq and the wider Arab world. Aiming for calm at home and new friends abroad, he failed to secure either, alienating the UAR through his refusal to join the federation while stirring up Kurdish hostility by going back on his promise to afford the Kurds greater autonomy.

Narrowly surviving an assassination attempt by members of the Ba'ath Party in late 1959 (thanks to a young Saddam Hussein literally jumping the gun by shooting too early and throwing the whole enterprise into disarray), Qasim suffered another setback in 1961 when the Kurds, led by Mustafa Barzani, revolted. Undermined militarily and loathed by many officers due to several purges, Qasim's luck ran out in 1963 when his former co-conspirator Colonel Abdul Salam Arif launched the Ramadan Revolution.

Allegedly helped by the CIA, Arif was in no mood to be merciful. Despite Qasim reminding Arif that Qasim had commuted Arif's death sentence when he was imprisoned in 1959 for plotting against his former co-revolutionary, Arif didn't feel any obligation or indeed inclination to return the favour. Ignoring Qasim's increasingly desperate pleas to be spared, he indulged in a show trial before

*Staring down the barrel: soldiers loyal to Abdul Arif drive a tank through the streets of Baghdad in the wake of the Ramadan Revolution*

# LIQUID GOLD

The story of the search for oil beneath the deserts of the Middle East is, fittingly, a murky tale. It begins with a man named William Knox D'Arcy, a businessman who made himself fantastically wealthy through mining ventures in New Zealand and Australia. In 1901, he signed the D'Arcy Concession with the Shah of Persia, securing him the right to explore for oil in the region. It proved an expensive waste of his time and resources, and by the time he was appointed director of the Anglo-Persian Oil Company (which would later become BP), D'Arcy was bankrupt. A few years later, in 1912, the Turkish Petroleum Company, a conglomerate of British, American, French and Dutch oil companies that would later be renamed the Iraqi Petroleum Company, was formed. In 1925 it was granted a 75-year concession to look for oil in exchange for the Iraqi Government receiving a royalty on every ton extracted. Oil was struck in Baba Gurgur in October 1927. In response, the members of the TPC signed the Red Line Agreement, the terms of which gave each of the four companies a 23.75 per cent share of all the oil the TPC produced (the other five per cent was to be given to an Armenian stakeholder called Calouste Gulbenkian). It also stipulated that the companies would not develop oilfields within the territory comprising the TPC without consent from the other members. When Abd al-Karim Qasim staged his coup in 1958 he demanded better terms from this oil cartel, and in 1961 Iraq passed Public Law 80 to enable the government to take 95 per cent of the IPC's concessions. It also founded the Iraq National Oil Company with a view to developing the assets stripped from the IPC. It then nationalised the IPC in 1972, cementing the government's grip on Iraq's oil.

members of the Ba'ath Party shot Qasim in the Ministry of Defence building.

A political chameleon, Arif soon turned on his Ba'athist backers. When the Syrian branch of the party toppled their government in 1963, Arif initiated talks with Syria and Egypt about a potential union (a 1961 coup in Syria had resulted in the collapse of the UAR). However, when negotiations broke down after President Gamal Nasser of Egypt lambasted the Syrian Ba'athists for purging Nasserist officers, Arif pounced on the rapidly widening divisions within the party and forced the majority of the Ba'athists out of government.

Refusing to admit defeat, the Ba'athists plotted to remove Arif. Among the schemers were Saddam Hussein and his cousin Ahmed Hassan al-Bakr. Both would receive prison terms when their plot was discovered, but in 1966 Saddam escaped prison. That same year Arif died in a helicopter crash. His son Abdul assumed the presidency, but in 1968 the Ba'athists finally succeeded, taking power without a shot being fired. Al-Bakr became the fourth President of Iraq, securing control in large part thanks to Saddam's efforts to reshape the party after his appointment as its

Deputy Secretary of Regional Command. His rise to the top had begun.

In need of a major backer on the global stage, Ba'athist Iraq turned to the USSR. For their part, the communists (whose Iraqi followers were once persecuted) wanted to prevent the US gaining influence in the Middle East. In 1972, Iraq and the USSR signed a 15-year treaty of "friendship and cooperation", one that saw Soviet arms flooding into Iraq. Some of these weapons were used to finally put an end to the Kurdish revolt, which was finished off by the 1975 Algiers Agreement, a deal between Iran and Iraq that, among other issues, finally settled the Shatt al-Arab dispute that had raged on and off since 1936.

This strategically crucial waterway was used by both nations to export oil, and the struggle to control it exploded into open warfare in 1974. After over 1,000 people died in the fighting, Iraq agreed to acquiesce to Iran's demands over the precise demarcation of the Shatt al-Arab in return for Tehran ending its support of the Kurdish rebels. In one fell swoop a damaging inter-state entanglement and a bloody rebellion were ended. But the violence didn't stop there.

*An oil drilling tower in Kirkuk District in the north of Iraq in 1932. Iraq is today the fifth-largest exporter of oil*

# "DETERMINED TO MODERNISE IRAQ, FAISAL USED SOARING OIL PROFITS TO CONSTRUCT DAMS, BRIDGES, SCHOOLS AND HOSPITALS"

# LAND OF BLOOD AND OIL

## Riven by sectarian divisions and menaced from abroad, Iraq needed a saviour. It was given a tyrant

Like many countries, Iraq is a melting pot of cultures and creeds. However, unlike most of the Muslim world, the majority of its population are Shia. The rift between Sunni and Shia followers dates back almost 1,400 years and concerns the successors of the Prophet Muhammad. The Shia believe that the leader of the Muslim world should hail from Muhammad's bloodline, while the Sunnis claim the Prophet did not appoint a successor and that his followers chose Abu Bakr to be the first Caliph.

The majority of Iraq's Shia population were opposed to the idea of Pan-Arabism, as were the Kurds, with both wary of being marginalised in a wider Arab world dominated by Sunni nations. Unfortunately for the people of Iraq, a ruthlessly ambitious former rebel was destined to take power, a man with no qualms about resorting to the worst excesses in his thirst to rule.

On 16 July 1979, Saddam Hussein replaced his ailing cousin to become the fifth President of Iraq. Shaped by years of carnage and plotting, Saddam was wily enough to know how to build a loyal support network. Within weeks of assuming his new role he ordered the execution of hundreds of Ba'athists he deemed as being part of a "fifth column". A lot of the victims of the Khuld Purge were members of other religious or cultural groups, inflaming sectarianism.

Saddam appointed trusted friends and followers to positions of influence as he moved to impose a strict national identity. Disregarding the simmering sectarian tensions among the Kurds and ostracised Shia, he continued previous efforts to Arabise the north, further displacing the Kurds. Saddam also deported Shi'ites, Iranians and Kurds with the justification that they were foreigners. Everywhere Iraqis turned, they were closely monitored. The slightest hint of dissent was to be starved of oxygen.

The Iranian Revolution of 1978–79 propelled a firebrand named Ruhollah Khomeini to Iran's political summit, a lofty position from which he extolled the virtues of spreading revolutionary fervour along Shia lines. Prior to ousting the Shah of Iran (and thereby ending its monarchy), Khomeini had spent some time exiled in Iraq, where he made quite the impression. In April 1980, Iraqi admirers of the Ayatollah attempted to assassinate Prime Minister Tariq Aziz.

Khomeini was clearly a force to be reckoned with, but his overthrow of the Shah left the Iranian military demoralised and rudderless. Coupled with the PR disaster that was the Iran hostage crisis (in which 53 Americans were taken hostage inside the US embassy in Tehran by fanatical students), Iran was domestically weak and internationally isolated. Saddam required no better invitation.

Eyes set on making territorial gains and overturning the deal over the Shatt Al-Arab, in September 1980 Saddam rolled the dice and invaded a stunned Iran, much to the consternation of the international community, especially Iraq's Soviet allies.

Prior to the eruption of hostilities along the border, the Soviets enjoyed a mixed relationship with Iraq, exchanging oil for arms, sharing their military expertise and teaching the Iraqi secret police the dark arts of surveillance. Yet at no point did Iraq submit to the will of its colossal ally, a stubborn independence fully displayed when Saddam attacked Iran, who the Soviets had been trying to form ties with. Now the Soviets were forced to make a choice, one they attempted to avoid by declaring their "strict neutrality" and overall displeasure at the outbreak of war.

Try as they might, the Soviets couldn't hold to this position forever, and as Iran began to recover and launch successful counterattacks, the threat of Khomeini stirring up an Islamic revolution in Central Asia, and thereby jeopardising Soviet interests, led the USSR to ship over 20 billion dollars' worth of arms into Iraq, a mammoth influx that accounted for over 30 per cent of all military imports into the country. In time they would turn the tide of war.

After fighting Iran to a standstill and finally coming to terms in 1988, Saddam was in a

## "IRAN WAS DOMESTICALLY WEAK AND INTERNATIONALLY ISOLATED. SADDAM REQUIRED NO BETTER INVITATION"

*The economic cost of the war is estimated to have been well in excess of $500 billion*

A dapper Saddam Hussein is all smiles sitting beside Ahmed al-Bakr in this 1978 photo. Within a year Hussein would topple his cousin

vengeful mood, and his ire soon concentrated on a less well-known group: the Marsh Arabs.

This unique society of half a million people occupied a vast wetland situated in the south of Iraq on the floodplains of the Euphrates and Tigris rivers. Due to insurgents and members of persecuted groups seeking refuge in the reeds of this 12,000-square-mile ecosystem, many viewed the marshes, and therefore their people, with suspicion – none more so than Saddam, who accused them of harbouring criminals and assisting the Iranians. The price for their supposed treason was horrendous.

For no other purpose than to punish the Ma'dan (as the Marsh Arabs are also known), Saddam drained the marshes, destroying a delicate way of life centred around fishing, hunting, agriculture and tending to passing boats. Confronted with the loss of everything they held dear, most of the Ma'dan fled to Iran. The spring floods went with them, a vital ecological process blocked by dams. Yet although it cannot be argued that the treatment of the Ma'dan was cruel, it was not as depraved as the fate that would befall the Kurds. Citing their supposed betrayal of his regime (and not the fact that enormous oil reserves were found in the Kurdistan Region), Saddam continued his efforts to Arabise northern Iraq, which required the dislocation or, if necessary, extermination of the Kurds. Chastened by his failed assault on Iran, Saddam directed his wrath inwards in the shape of the Al-Anfal Campaign.

Throughout 1988, Kurds were detained, deported and murdered; around 90 per cent of villages and over 20 towns in the region were liquidated. One particular incident of occurred in the city of Halabja, where, at the behest of Ali Hassan al-Majid, better known as 'Chemical Ali', between 3,000–5,000 people were killed with mustard gas and nerve agents.

By September, it's thought around 100,000 Kurds had been murdered, part of an estimated 1 million who disappeared between the 1960s and the end of the Anfal Campaign in September 1988. It might seem incongruous that Saddam Hussein, a ruler who oversaw widespread religious tolerance (including towards both Jews and Christians), economic progress, a rise in women in employment, free tuition fees for students and a literacy drive hailed by UNESCO as "the most effective literacy campaign in the world" (albeit one backed up by the threat of imprisonment for failing to attend classes), could also order the cold-blooded killing of thousands of innocent people. But he was never above going as low as necessary to obtain what he wanted. In the summer of 1990, he would once again resort to violence in the name of Iraq's national interests. Once again, he'd bite off a lot more than he could chew.

# DEATH IN THE DESERT

Equipped with a vast arsenal of Soviet weaponry and a burning desire to enhance Iraq's territorial holdings, on 22 September 1980, Saddam Hussein unleashed his forces on neighbouring Iran, triggering an almost eight-year war that would kill as many as 2 million and leave the original border between the two countries in place. After making some initial gains, the Iraqi forces encountered hardening resistance. So intransigent were the Iranians that by 1982 Iraq withdrew its soldiers and sought peace, an offer Ayatollah Khomeini rejected. Demanding the overthrow of Saddam's regime, the Iranian leader continued the war, a decision that saw the Soviets move from a position of neutrality to openly backing Iraq's cause. Shipping around $9 billion in arms to Iraq, the Soviets supplied over 2,000 tanks, 300 fighter jets, a similar number of missiles and countless pieces of artillery and armoured vehicles. Reinvigorated, the Iraqis managed to halt the Iranian advance and both sides dug in (literally in the form of trenches) along the border for a protracted stalemate. In the summer of 1988 a series of Iraqi breakthroughs convinced Iran to come to the negotiating table, where both nations agreed to a ceasefire proposed by the UN. Although Saddam's hopes of humbling Iran were dashed, thanks to the backing of the majority of the Arab world during the conflict, coupled with a battle-hardened and better-armed military, he was in a strong position. Two years later he would send his armies back into the fray by invading Kuwait.

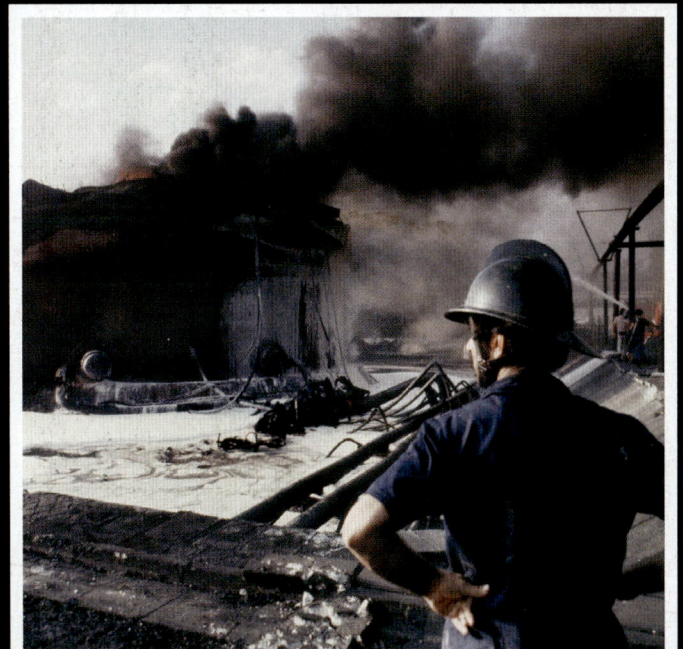

# THE INVASION OF
# KUWAIT

The Iraqi army struck suddenly and swiftly on 2 August, overwhelming the small number of Kuwaiti defenders and occupying the capital

WORDS: TIM WILLIAMSON

*There was public outcry following the invasion of Kuwait*

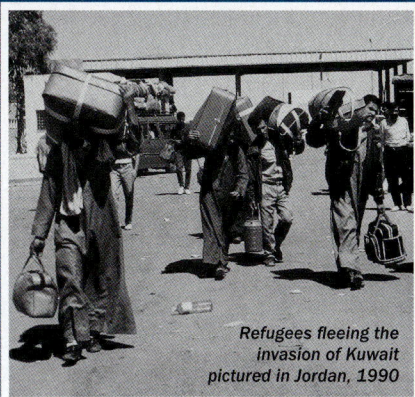

*Refugees fleeing the invasion of Kuwait pictured in Jordan, 1990*

*Saddam Hussein praying in the Kuwaiti desert after the August invasion*

In the early morning of 2 August, 1990, thousands of Iraqi forces began their assault on Kuwait over sea, land and air. It was a sudden, violent culmination of a heated war of words between the two Arabian states. For months, there had been increasing tension between Iraq and its tiny southern neighbour, including disputes over territory, unpaid loans and, perhaps most contentiously, oil. Buoyed by the small successes of his bloody war with Iran, but faced with a ravaged economy, President Saddam Hussein's rhetoric towards Kuwait turned from belligerent to hostile by the summer of 1990. Meanwhile, the international community looked on with apprehension at the prospect of a conflict over the world's second-largest oil field. Despite this backdrop, the Kuwaiti military was caught almost entirely by surprise when armoured columns and attack helicopters were reported storming across the border overnight. Four divisions of the Republican Guard – Saddam's most loyal, best-equipped and professional units – formed the bulk of the more than 100,000-strong invasion force, alongside special forces and marines. The Kuwaiti defenders counted barely a fifth of their enemy's number, though fielded a number of British-made Chieftain tanks, which could more than match Iraq's T-72s for firepower. Despite facing overwhelming odds, there were pockets of fierce Kuwaiti resistance that achieved some tactical victories. West of Kuwait City, near the town of Al Jahra, Kuwait's 35th Armoured Brigade engaged two advancing Iraqi columns, from the Hammurabi and Medina divisions. In what afterwards became known as the Battle of the Bridges, Kuwaiti Chieftain tanks engaged the Iraqi columns, inflicting heavy losses and slowing their advance towards the capital. At risk of being surrounded, the 35th was forced to withdraw south, eventually crossing the border into Saudi Arabia. They were among the 7,000 or so Kuwaiti forces that were able to escape and continue the fight during the subsequent coalition operations – the remaining defenders were killed, captured, or went to ground.

One of the main Iraqi objectives on day one of the invasion was the grand Dasman Palace, residence of Kuwait's leader, Emir Jaber Al-Ahmad Al-Sabah. The Iraqis intended to capture the Emir and his inner circle, however they had already fled to neighbouring Saudi Arabia soon after reports of the Iraqi offensive reached them. A small number of Kuwaiti royal guards, led by the Emir's brother Fahd Al-Ahmad, remained behind to defend the palace, which by the afternoon of 2 August was captured by the Iraqis.

*Iraqi forces pictured on a Kuwaiti street shortly after the beginning of the Iraqi occupation of the country*

*The UN Security Council in session, 6 August 1990, voted for Resolution 661 placing strict sanctions on Iraq*

# THE UN RESPONDS

When news of the invasion spread around the globe, the United Nations Security Council gathered for an emergency session, the first of many galvanising the international response

**WORDS: TIM WILLIAMSON**

*An American woman protests with crowds in Paris against the Gulf War*

*Protestors gather outside the United Nations building in New York, November 1990*

*US president George HW Bush was a driving force in the international community's response to the invasion of Kuwait*

When reports confirmed the Iraqi offensive on 2 August, the United Nations Security Council voted overwhelmingly in condemnation of the invasion in an emergency session, with only Yemen abstaining. In addition, Resolution 660 – the first of several votes on the Iraqi invasion – called for an immediate withdrawal of Iraqi forces, and the beginning of negotiations between the two sides. As the days passed, it became clear that Iraq was not only unwilling to comply and negotiate with Kuwait, it was determined to remove the tiny nation from existence altogether. Immediately following the short and brutal invasion, with only limited Kuwaiti resistance still present, Saddam installed the Provisional Government of Free Kuwait. Supposedly born of a popular Kuwaiti revolutionary movement, in reality it was a puppet regime.

On 8 August Iraq declared that "a comprehensive and eternal merger" had taken place between the two countries – in effect announcing Kuwait was now Iraq. Saddam installed his cousin, the ruthless Ali Hassan al-Majid as its governor. At the same time, the first US troops arrived in Saudi Arabia. The next day, all 15 members of the UN council voted for Resolution 662 declaring Iraq's annexation of Kuwait illegal, and repeating its demands for the occupation to end.

Over the following weeks and months, eight further resolutions were passed by the council, placing sanctions on Iraqi goods, and any exports from occupied Kuwait. Resolutions were also passed calling for the protection and release of foreign nationals in Iraq and Kuwait, including many diplomats, who along with their families had been seized after the invasion. They were reportedly being held hostage in key strategic locations across the country, as what were described as human shields, to deter military action against Saddam's forces.

On 29 November, a final decisive vote was held on whether action could be taken by UN members in order to enforce all its previous resolutions on Iraq. Resolution 678 was passed with two votes against, from Cuba and Yemen. The wording of the resolution stated "all means necessary" could be used in order to restore peace and security in the region.

"The UN Security Council has endorsed 12 resolutions to condemn Iraq's unprovoked invasion and occupation of Kuwait…" President George Bush declared in a speech the day after the critical vote. "Forces of 26 other nations are standing shoulder to shoulder with our troops in the Gulf. The fact is that it is not the United States against Iraq, it is Iraq against the world."

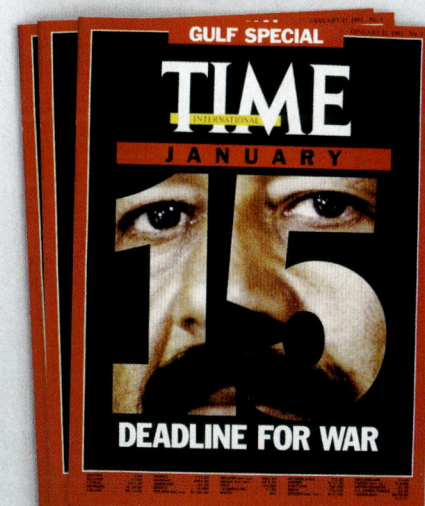

*A Time magazine cover depicts Saddam Husseum among the looming 15 January deadline set by the UN*

# A GLOBAL COALITION

**Saddam Hussein's Iraq had to fight a truly international alliance of 36 contributing nations dominated by the United States**

*Secretary of Defence Dick Cheney meets with Sultan bin Abdulaziz Al Saud in Saudi Arabia*

At the beginning of Operation Desert Storm, Iraq had – on paper – formidable armed forces. It had invaded Kuwait in 1990 with 100,000 men and in 1991 it mobilised all of its reserves, which boosted numbers to over 600,000 troops. However, it faced a numerically and technically superior UN coalition that had been formed by the United Nations' Security Council Resolution 678 in November 1990. Dominated by the United States but including 36 countries, the Coalition was an overwhelmingly huge force of almost one million personnel, thousands of aircraft and tanks, and hundreds of ships.

One sense of the scale of the Coalition was the war's projected costs. The US Department of Defense estimated the cost at $61 million, with America's allies contributing approximately $54 million. Of the latter sum, the main contributors were Saudi Arabia and other Gulf states, while Germany and Japan also provided substantial amounts of money. In purely military terms, the Coalition was overwhelmingly American with almost 700,000 personnel. By comparison, the second and third biggest pools of manpower, Saudi Arabia and the United Kingdom, contributed approximately 94,000 and 53,000 troops respectively. The Coalition threw together unlikely allies such as Argentina and Britain who had fiercely clashed during the Falklands War less than ten years before. Middle Eastern and Asian countries, some of whom would become heavily destabilised during the following two decades, also participated. Egypt and Morocco, who had been at war in the 1960s, combined forces while Syria provided approximately 21,000 troops. Even Afghanistan, which had only just concluded the Soviet-Afghan War, provided 300 Mujahideen fighters for the Coalition. Most of the other Coalition allies provided military personnel that numbered in their hundred, with the smallest being Hungary, who provided one 40-strong medical team.

Perhaps the most surprising ally was the recently unified Germany. Although they were a major financial contributor, the Germans had not undertaken a military role since WWII. Nevertheless, a Bundeswehr Luftwaffe fighter squadron provided logistical support from Turkey, which quietly reintroduced Germany as a military power.

*Coalition troops from Egypt, France, Oman, Syria and Kuwait stand for a review by King Fahd of Saudi Arabia, 8 March 1991*

*A multinational group of aircraft from Qatar, France, Canada and the United States fly in formation during Operation Desert Storm*

# IRAQ VERSUS THE COALITION

## THE MOST CONTRIBUTING ALLIED COUNTRIES THAT FOUGHT SADDAM'S FORCES

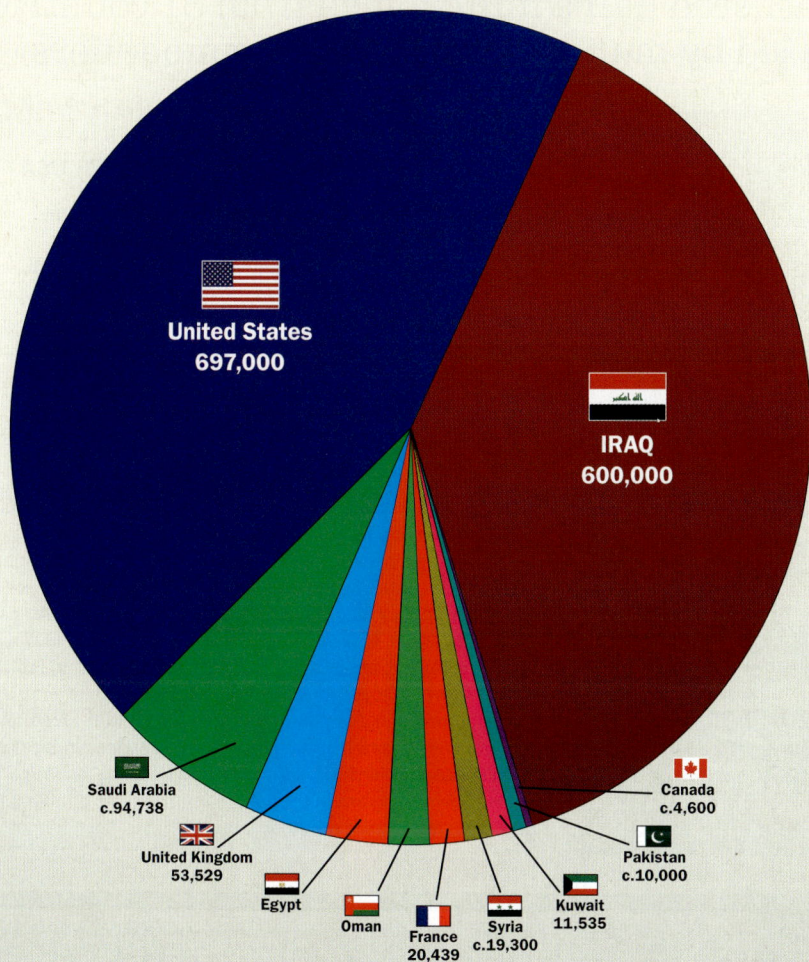
Captured Iraqi tanks on show in Kuwait after the end of the Gulf War

**United States
697,000**

**IRAQ
600,000**

Saudi Arabia
c.94,738

Canada
c.4,600

United Kingdom
53,529

Pakistan
c.10,000

Egypt

Oman

France
20,439

Syria
c.19,300

Kuwait
11,535

| | PERSONNEL | TANKS | AIRCRAFT | SHIPS |
|---|---|---|---|---|
| IRAQ | 600,000 | c.1,900 | 300 | c.33 |
| UNITED STATES | 697,000 | 2,000 | 1,940 | 271 |
| SAUDI ARABIA | c.94,000 | 550 | 180 | 8 |
| UNITED KINGDOM | 53,000 | 455 | 58 | 16 |
| EGYPT | c.40,000 | 400 | 0 | 0 |
| OMAN | c.25,500 | 75 | 50 | 12 |
| FRANCE | 20,000 | 350 | 75 | 14 |
| SYRIA | c.19,000 | 300 | 0 | 0 |
| KUWAIT | 11,500 | 0 | 35 | 0 |
| PAKISTAN | c.10,000 | 0 | 0 | 0 |
| CANADA | c.4,600 | 0 | 0 | 0 |

## HONOURABLE MENTIONS

### COALITION'S OTHER CONTRIBUTORS

| COUNTRY | 1 2 3 4 5 |
|---|---|
| United Arab Emirates | 4,300 |
| Qatar | 2,600 |
| Bangladesh | 2,300 |
| Morocco | 2,000 |
| Italy | 1,950 |
| Australia | 700 |
| Netherlands | 700 |
| Niger | 600 |
| Sweden | 525 |
| Senegal | 500 |
| Spain | 500 |
| Argentina | 450 |
| Bahrain | 400 |
| Belgium | 400 |
| Czechoslovakia | 350 |
| Poland | 319 |
| South Korea | 314 |
| Afghanistan | 300 |
| Norway | 280 |
| Greece | 200 |
| Philippines | 200 |
| Honduras | 150 |
| Denmark | 100 |
| New Zealand | 100 |
| Germany | 1 fighter squadron |
| Hungary | 40 |

# LEADERS & COMMANDERS

In 1990 the US-led Coalition gathered half a million men from 31 countries in Saudi Arabia. They were led by multinational senior commanders

*General Norman Schwarzkopf Coalition commander-in-chief*

## GENERAL H. NORMAN SCHWARZKOPF

**COALITION FORCES COMMANDER-IN-CHIEF, *USA***

By 1990 Schwarzkopf was a highly experienced combat commander. Born in Trenton, New Jersey he was commissioned as a second lieutenant in 1956. He served in Vietnam first as an advisor to the Army of the Republic of Vietnam and then a battalion commander with the 6th Infantry. He was wounded four times in 1966 while leading an ARVN assault against the Viet Cong. In 1983 as a major general, he was deputy commander of Joint Task Force 120 under Vice Admiral Joseph Metcalf III. This conducted Operation Urgent Fury, the invasion of Grenada designed to drive out Cuban troops. This was notable because it signalled renewed confidence by the US military for overseas expeditions following the humiliation of Vietnam. Five years later Schwarzkopf assumed command of US Central Command or CENTCOM based in Tampa, Florida, with responsibility for American military operations in the Middle East, North Africa and Central Asia. In his role as Coalition commander he was supported by Lieutenant General John Yeostock, commanding the US Army deployed for Desert Shield, Vice Admiral Stan Arthur commanding the US naval forces in the Gulf, Lieutenant General Walt Boomer commanding the US Marines in the Gulf and Lieutenant Chuck Horner commanding the US Air Force in the region. Schwarzkopf returned to America as a national hero and shortly after retired to write his bestselling memoir *It Doesn't Take A Hero*.

## LIEUTENANT GENERAL PRINCE KHALID BIN SULTAN AL SAUD

**SAUDI COMMANDER OF THE JOINT ARAB FORCES, *SAUDI ARABIA***

Khalid graduated from King Saud University. In the late 1960s he attended the Royal Military Academy Sandhurst. He also trained at the US Army's Command and General Staff College at Fort Leavenworth, Kansas. He then graduated from the Air War College at Maxwell Air Force Base, Alabama. Back in Saudi Arabia he oversaw the acquisition of guided missiles from China and then created the Saudi Air Defense Force, which he commanded. During Operation Desert Sabre he commanded Joint Forces Command North, consisting of units from Saudi Arabia, Egypt and Syria. Schwarzkopf noted, "His military credentials were nowhere near as important as his princely blood, since almost all power in Saudi Arabia resides in an inner circle of the Royal family. Simply put, unlike other generals Khalid had the authority to write checks." After the war he retired and later became the Saudi Minister of Defense. Subsequently he commanded Saudi Arabia's controversial military intervention in neighbouring Yemen.

*General Prince Khalid commander of the Joint Arab forces*

# GENERAL CHARLES 'CHUCK' HORNER

### LED AMERICAN & ALLIED AIR FORCES DURING DESERT STORM USA

General Charles Horner joined the United States Air Force as a pilot in the late 1950s and flew numerous combat missions during the Vietnam War. By the late 1980s he had been appointed commander of the US Ninth Air Force as well as commander of CENTCOM's air forces. In the Gulf he initially acted as commander-in-chief until the arrival of General Schwarzkopf. His task was to degrade the Iraqi armed forces occupying Kuwait and in southern Iraq to a point where they would be unable to resist Schwarzkopf's ground offensive. The air campaign, known as Desert Storm, did this with great effect. He retired in 1994.

*General Chuck Horner marching in the Welcome Home parade in New York City*

*Source: Wiki / PD Gov*

# GENERAL SIR PETER DE LA BILLIÈRE

### BRITISH FORCES LEADER IN THE GULF UK

Peter de la Billière joined the British Army as a private in 1952, and was subsequently commissioned as a second lieutenant with the Durham Light Infantry. In the mid-1950s he joined the SAS seeing action in Malaya and Oman and Borneo. He became the regiment's director in 1979. Although due to retire de la Billière assumed command of the British Forces in the Middle East on 6 October 1990. Under his command the UK contingent grew from 14,000 men in November 1990 to more than 45,000 by the time the war against Iraq came to an end. His key unit was the British 1st Armoured Division commanded by Major General Rupert Smith. The division comprised the 4th and 7th Armoured Brigades under Brigadiers Christopher Hammerbeck and Patrick Cordingley. He retired after the war receiving the American Legion of Merit, Canadian Meritorious Service Cross and the Saudi Order of King Abdulaziz for his services.

*General Peter de la Billière the British forces commander*

© Alamy

# LIEUTENANT GENERAL MICHEL ROQUEJEOFFRE

### COMMANDER OF THE FRENCH RAPID REACTION FORCE, FRANCE

Michel Roquejeoffre attended the premier French military academy at Sain-Cyr in 1952. He saw active service in Cambodia, Chad, Lebanon and Algeria. In Saudi Arabia his forces comprised Foreign Legion, Marine infantry, helicopter and armoured car units. His main strike formation was the French 6th Light Armoured Division commanded by Brigadier General Bernard Janvier. There was some concern they would not take part in the ground war, but Roquejeoffre did commit his troops to protect the Americans' far flank. Schwarzkopf liked Roquejeoffre noting "whom I respected and counted as a friend". He was awarded the Legion of Merit by America for his services in the Gulf.

*Lieutenant General Michel Roquejeoffre led the French Rapid Reaction Force*

*Source: Wiki / PD Gov*

# BRIGADIER PATRICK CORDINGLEY

### DESERT RATS COMMANDER UK

Patrick Cordingley joined the British Army in 1963 and two years later was commissioned into the 5th Royal Dragoon Guards. He saw service in Libya, Cyprus, Germany and Canada before teaching at the British Staff College. Then in 1988 he took command of the 7th Armoured Brigade – the famed Desert Rats. During the Gulf War his brigade fought the Iraqi 12th Armoured Division and the 48th Infantry Division capturing a series of positions dubbed Copper and Zinc. In the opening battles they knocked out almost 60 Iraqi armoured vehicles. After the war he was promoted to major general and commanded the British 2nd Division based in York. During which time he wrote *In The Eye Of The Storm* an account of his experiences in the Gulf War. He retired in 2000.

*Desert Rats commander Brigadier Cordingley*

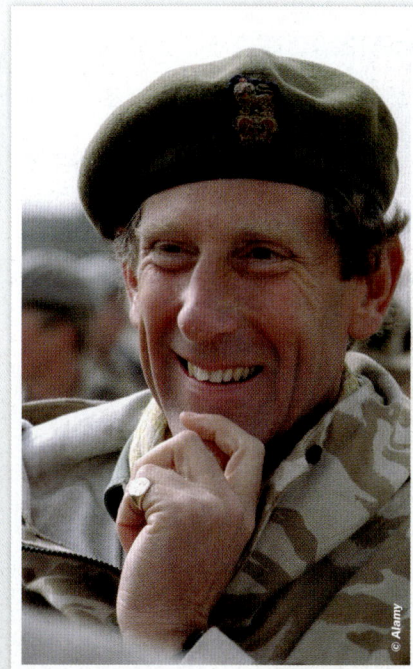

© Alamy

# SADDAM HUSSEIN

## Discover how a nationalist revolutionary from a broken home rose to supreme power in Iraq and became a bellicose opponent of the West

**WORDS: SCOTT REEVES**

The baby born to Subha Tulfah al-Mussallat in the Iraqi village of al-Awja in April 1937 was named Saddam – Arabic for 'one who confronts'. It would prove to be a suitable name for the newest member of a family in turmoil.

Saddam's father, Hussein 'Abd al-Majid, abandoned the family six months previously and never saw his son. Nor would Saddam remember his 13-year-old brother, who died from cancer shortly after he was born. For three years, Saddam lived with an uncle, Khairallah Talfah, who was a devout Sunni Muslim and fierce nationalist, but he was returned to his newly remarried mother when Talfah was imprisoned for his role in a rebellion against the British in 1941. However, Hussein's new stepfather treated him harshly and, at the age of 10, he ran away to rejoin his uncle shortly after Talfah was released from prison.

Similarly to the Hussein family, the country of Iraq was also in a state of unrest. Arab nationalist movements were growing and Hussein was influenced by his uncle Talfah, choosing to join the Arab nationalist Ba'ath Party at the age of 20. The following year, King Faisal II was overthrown and a republic declared. Although the Ba'athists initially supported General Qasim's coup, they quickly turned against him due to his failure to join Nasser's United Arab Republic, a short-lived union of Egypt and Syria.

Saddam first rose to prominence during a Ba'athist assassination attempt on the life of Qasim on 7 October 1959. It failed, possibly due to the fact that one of the assassins – a young,

## SADDAM'S SONS

Saddam intended that the Hussein family would continue to rule Iraq after his death. Initially his elder son, Uday, was the favoured successor. However, he was infamous for his criminal behaviour, including rape and murder. Uday survived an assassination attempt in 1996, but his slow rehabilitation gave his father an opportunity to sideline the loose cannon.

In 2000, Saddam named his second son, Qusay, as his new successor. He was appointed to run the elite Iraqi Republican Guard and Special Security Organisation, and entrusted to carry out the brutal repression of Marsh Arab and Shia rebellions. After the fall of their father's regime in 2003, both Uday and Qusay were killed in a six-hour firefight.

trigger-happy recruit named Saddam Hussein – opened fire on the President's car prematurely. Despite Qasim escaping with his life, Saddam's role in the assassination attempt would later be lionised in propaganda: he is said to have held the operation together in the confusion that followed, gouging a bullet from his own flesh before trekking across the country to safety in Syria.

Saddam spent four years in exile, only returning to Iraq in 1963 after Qasim was deposed and executed in a Ba'ath coup, but a second coup followed at the end of the year during which the new president, Abdul Salam Arif, purged his government of many Ba'athists. Saddam was arrested and imprisoned, accused of planning another presidential assassination attempt.

Escaping prison in 1966, Saddam began a rapid rise through the Ba'ath Party ranks. He was elected to the Iraqi Regional Command of the party, and soon after appointed Deputy Secretary. When the Ba'ath Party split into separate Iraqi and Syrian elements, Saddam created and controlled the Ba'ath security service. Within two years, the Iraqi Ba'aths led another coup that overthrew President Abdul Rahman Arif, who had replaced his brother as president. Saddam escorted Prime Minister Abd ar-Razzaq an-Naif out of the country at gunpoint – despite al-Naif actually supporting the coup – and was named Deputy President of Iraq.

Considering the tumult of the past decade, the next few years saw Saddam bring about a remarkable period of political stability and economic growth. He nationalised international oil interests in Iraq on 1 June 1972 – a fortuitous

*Saddam Hussein, here with Egyptian president Hosni Mubarak, sought support across the Arab world in his conflicts with Iran and the West*

decision considering that prices rocketed the following year during the 1973 Oil Crisis. Enormous wealth poured into the country, with annual oil revenues rising from less than a half billion dollars to tens of billions, allowing Saddam to implement a social security programme that was unprecedented in the Middle East: free schooling helped to bring illiteracy rates tumbling down and free healthcare improved life expectancy, leading to Saddam being given an award by UNESCO. New roads were built, new industries were encouraged with state aid, and agriculture was modernised. Saddam had become

*The 1980 invasion of Iran soon descended into a vicious war of attrition that lasted nearly eight years*

indispensable, even more so as the health of the elderly president, Ahmed Hassan al-Bakr, began to fail. When al-Bakr resigned on 16 July 1979, Saddam was the only real choice as his successor. Yet within days, Saddam signalled that he would be ruthless in his quest to retain power. In a meeting of Ba'ath Party leaders on 22 July, he announced that he had discovered a treasonous plot within the party, and had 68 people in the room immediately arrested. Some were executed by firing squad; the other alleged conspirators were forced to fire the guns. Hundreds more Ba'athists were targeted over the next few days until Saddam was happy that those who

# OPERATION
# DESERT STORM

## WHAT BEGAN AS A CONFLICT OVER OIL PRICES SPIRALLED INTO THE DEADLY FIRST GULF WAR - A HUMILIATING LOSS FOR IRAQ

Perhaps Saddam Hussein expected the world to stand aside when he invaded Kuwait in 1990, but the response of the UN was to launch military action. Led by US President George HW Bush and UK Prime Minister Margaret Thatcher, a coalition of 35 countries embarked on a campaign to free Kuwait of the occupying Iraqis.

A five-week aerial and naval bombardment commenced on 17 January 1991, with camera footage of laser-guided bombs destroying their targets broadcast around the world. The Iraqi response was to fire Scud missiles into Israel, hoping to provoke an Israeli retaliation that could potentially lead to Arab countries withdrawing from the Coalition. However, the Israelis did not strike back and a coalition ground campaign began on 24 February. Kuwait was swiftly freed, although the Iraqi troops set fire to 700 oil wells in a scorched-earth retreat. The advance lasted for only 100 hours. With Kuwait liberated, the Coalition's objectives had been met and a ceasefire was declared, bringing the conflict came to an end. Although Iraq had been decisively defeated, Saddam was allowed to remain in power and would continue to rule Iraq with an iron fist until another US-led coalition returned in 2003, this time under a different President Bush.

The Coalition's air superiority meant that Iraq was unable to put up any serious resistance

The toppling of Saddam's statue in the centre of Baghdad marked a symbolic end to his rule – although the dictator himself had already fled

remained after the bloodbaths were entirely loyal to him and him alone.

Throughout the rest of his 24-year presidency, terror was his first and foremost method of dealing with dissent. The Department of General Intelligence – or Mukhabarat – was commanded by Saddam's younger half-brother. In 1983, when 18 members of Ayatollah Mohammad Baqir al-Hakim's family were executed to intimidate the exiled senior Shia cleric into silence, it was the Mukhabarat who were responsible. In 1982, more than 140 people were executed in Dujail in reprisal for an assassination attempt on Saddam. In total as many as 250,000 Iraqis may have been killed by their own government.

Saddam fostered a cult of personality, with countless portraits, posters, statues and murals displayed throughout the country. He would be portrayed in different ways to appeal to the various ethnic groups who called Iraq home: in the traditional clothes of the Iraqi peasant, as a modern urban statesman in tailored suits, in Muslim headdress and robes, even in traditional Kurdish clothing. To demonstrate his appeal, Saddam ordered two referendums to be held on his leadership. The first, in 1995, saw him receive 99.96 per cent of the votes in a 99.47 per cent turnout. In the second, on 15 October 2002, every single one of the 11,445,638 ballots recorded a positive vote for the incumbent president – there was not even a single example of a spoiled or invalid paper.

Saddam may have held Iraq in a steely grip, but his eventual downfall stemmed from an overly aggressive foreign policy. In the same year that Saddam became President of Iraq, the Iranian

Saddam developed a cult of personality with paintings, posters and statues depicting him as Iraq's protector

Saddam's invasion of Kuwait would prove to be a strategic error, with the Iraqi forces no match for the US-led coalition

## "SADDAM ORDERED CHEMICAL WEAPONS TO BE USED ON THE IRANIAN FRONT AND AGAINST KURDISH SEPARATISTS IN IRAQ"

Revolution saw the Shah replaced by Ayatollah Ruhollah Khomeini. Saddam and Khomeini already had a strained relationship, and conflict between Sunni Iraq and Shia Iran seemed inevitable. It was Saddam who struck first. On 22 September 1980, Iraqi troops crossed the border and invaded their neighbour, hoping to seize the oil-rich territory of Khuzestan. However, despite diplomatic backing from the USA, Europe and much of the Arab world, the war descended into a long battle of attrition. Saddam ordered chemical weapons to be used on the Iranian front and against Kurdish separatists in Iraq. When the Kurdish town of Habalja was targeted by mustard gas and nerve agents, up to 5,000 civilians died.

The stalemate came to an end after nearly eight years. The border had barely moved, but half a million people had been killed and the once-burgeoning Iraqi economy was left in tatters. Tensions increased with Kuwait, a small but wealthy nation to Iraq's south-east. This was because diplomatic pressure to persuade the Emir to write off $30 billion of debts to Iraq failed, while the country also led opposition to Saddam's plan to cut oil exports across the Middle East to force up the price. The deterioration in relations led Saddam to invade Kuwait on 1 August 1990, claiming it as a province of Iraq.

Perhaps he hoped the USA and her European allies would allow him to get away with it – they had, after all, backed Iraq during the Iranian War, and considered Kuwait to be opposed to the controversial state of Israel. However, a US-led Coalition began air strikes against Iraq in January 1991, followed by a ground invasion. Outnumbered and outclassed, Saddam's armies suffered a comprehensive defeat. Saddam, however, was allowed to retain the presidency. Domestic insurrections went unsupported by the Coalition and were ruthlessly quashed. Economic sanctions caused hardship for Iraqis, but Saddam maintained absolute power just as firmly as he had before the conflict. He even gained support from many Arabs who decried Western interference in the Middle East.

Saddam would rule for 12 more years, and human rights abuses continued to be catalogued in Iraq, but not until after the 9/11 terrorist attacks in the USA was the Western world prepared to intervene again. President George W Bush included Iraq in his 'axis of evil' and declared that Saddam had a secret stash of weapons of mass destruction. With war looming, a worried Saddam cooperated with UN inspectors, and no evidence of prohibited weapons was found.

That did not stop a US-led coalition invading Iraq on 20 March 2003. Just as in the 1991 war, Iraqi resistance crumbled in the face of a superior foe, but unlike in 1991, this time the coalition pressed on in a quest to enact regime change. Baghdad fell within three weeks, but Saddam Hussein survived on the run until 13 December.

The former dictator, now sporting a beard, was plucked from a hole in the ground near ad-Dawr, a short distance from his birthplace. After being interrogated by US forces for six months, he was handed over to Iraqi authorities. They decided to prosecute him for the massacre in Dujail and, despite Saddam refusing to accept the court's authority, he was found guilty.

On 30 December 2006, the first day of Eid al-Adha, Hussein was hanged at an Iraqi Army base near Baghdad. Grainy mobile phone footage of the execution and its aftermath suggest that Saddam died amid a barrage of insults, that the hanging itself was botched, leaving Saddam with a wound in his neck, and that he may have been stabbed post-mortem. It was a humiliating end for the once-mighty dictator of Iraq.

Saddam's six months on the run came to an end near his birthplace

# IRAQ'S ELITE REPUBLICAN GUARD

WORDS: TIM WILLIAMSON

Saddam's loyal and best-equipped divisions were on the frontline of the invasion, and formed the last line of defence during the Coalition attack

Iraq's Republican Guard has often been referred to as Saddam's own Praetorian cohorts – his elite soldiers, but also loyal bodyguards. Formed initially as one brigade in the 1960s, during the Iran-Iraq War (1980-88) the Guard rapidly expanded and was deployed behind the main Iraqi army, serving as a mobile reserve. By the end of the war, the Guards divisions were on the frontline during the final Iraqi offensives to recapture lost territory from Iranian forces.

Not only battle-hardened by the long conflict with Iran, the Guard were also the best-equipped of Iraq's divisions, armed with air-defence units, self-propelled howitzers and specially modified T-72 tanks. Its recruits were also better paid, better supplied and officers were picked for their personal loyalty to Saddam – many were reportedly recruited from the president's home city of Tikrit to enhance their connection to their leader.

Four divisions were tasked with the invasion of Kuwait in August 1990: the Hammurabi and Medinah Armored Divisions, the Tawakalna Mechanised Infantry Division, as well as three brigades of the Guards' special forces, that were inserted into Kuwait City via helicopters. Four Guards infantry divisions were deployed as a second wave to secure the expected gains of the initial attack.

After the fall of Kuwait, the Guard were redeployed into southern Iraq, close to the border with Kuwait, and one division was kept in the capital Baghdad in order to protect the government – from domestic as well as foreign threats. During the months prior to Desert Storm, they prepared strong defensive positions, stocking up on ammunition and supplies for the coming battles.

During their planning, US commanders identified the Republican Guard as a key target for defeating the Iraqi Army, as well as a key threat to its ground and air forces. During the weeks-long aerial bombing campaign the Guards divisions in particular were targeted, sustaining heavy losses prior to the ground offensive. Though entrenched and well-concealed Guards units did put up stiff resistance to the Coalition ground forces, achieving some limited successes, they were ultimately destroyed or forced to escape the Coalition pincer from the west. Several divisions, including the Tawakalna Division were so severely weakened that they were disbanded. After the end of the Gulf War, remnants of the shattered Guards divisions were reorganised and immediately deployed to put down the 1991 uprisings against Saddam's regime.

The Republican Guard's T-72 tanks used well-prepared defensive positions to repel coalition forces, but were ultimately defeated

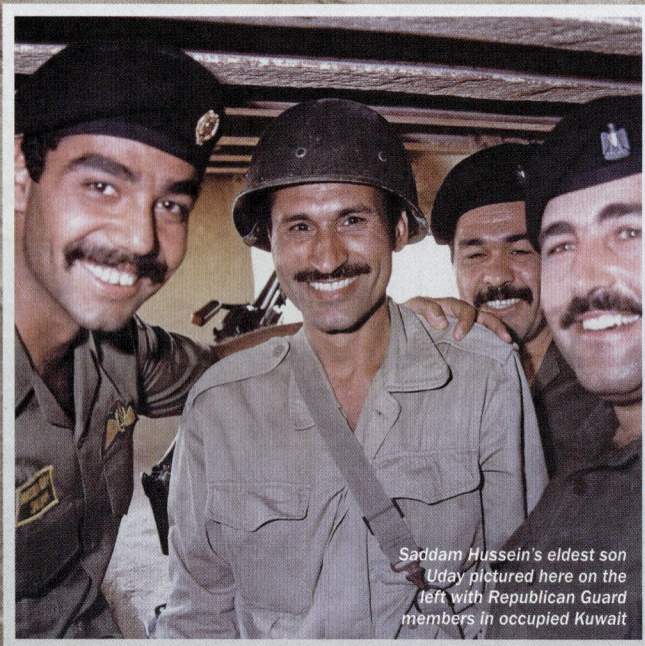

Saddam Hussein's eldest son Uday pictured here on the left with Republican Guard members in occupied Kuwait

Images:Getty Images, Alamy

A member of the Iraqi Republican Guard surrendering at a US checkpoint in April 1991

# OPERATION DESERT SHIELD

As Iraq's forces poured into Kuwait, an international Coalition formed to ensure the safety of other neighbouring countries, especially Saudi Arabia

**WORDS:** STUART HADAWAY

In August 1990 the world began to react to Saddam Hussein's unprovoked invasion of Kuwait. In several ways, Saddam chose the worst possible time for this attack. The recent ending of the Cold War gave the countries of NATO and the former Warsaw Pact a level of freedom to move and redeploy massive forces that they had not seen for half a century, while at the same time one of Iraq's biggest supporters, the Soviet Union, had to slash their own commitments. The principle Western military organisation in the region was the US Central Command (CENTOM) under General Norman Schwarzkopf. Long convinced of the danger that Saddam posed to the region, Schwarzkopf had drawn up a plan for the defence of Saudi Arabia early in 1990, Operation Plan 1002-90, and had war-gamed the scenario at his Florida headquarters in July, with the exercise ending just one week before the Iraqi invasion. Schwarzkopf and his staff were able to react quickly and efficiently, and on 9 August 1990 CENTCOM headquarters and leading troop elements landed at Dhahran and began to deploy north along the Kuwaiti border.

However, the Iraqi armed forces were considerable in size and highly experienced from their recent long war with Iran. With one million men under arms, around 6,000 Main Battle Tanks (MBTs), 2,000 close-support helicopters, 10,000 anti-aircraft guns, 16,000 Surface-to-Air Missiles (SAMs), 900 aircraft, and known chemical weapons stocks, Iraq then fielded the fourth largest army and sixth largest air force in the world. However fast and well-practised the American response, they would need international help to counter them.

President George HW Bush authorised the immediate deployment of the XVIII Airborne Corps (82nd and 101st Airborne and 24th Infantry Divisions, and the 3rd Armoured Cavalry Regiment) and a range of US Air Force (USAF) and US Marine units to Saudi Arabia, followed later by VII Corps from Germany. The USS Dwight D. Eisenhower and USS Independence Carrier Groups were the first of six US carrier groups to enter the Persian Gulf to enforce UN sanctions. In the United Nations a series of 15 resolutions were passed to place import and export sanctions on Iraq, including UNSCR 678 on 29 November 1990, which gave Saddam a deadline of 15 January 1991 to evacuate his troops. With a clear international consensus and UN backing, and resisting calls from the US press and politicians to counterattack immediately, Schwarzkopf began to build up his forces and develop a Coalition for the defence of Saudi Arabia as Operation Desert Shield.

The Coalition faced considerable practical and political difficulties. Large forces were needed; there would be 700,000 US personnel alone, and 950,000 overall. Such numbers needed an extensive logistical network to enable them to operate. Military camps had to be built and airfields expanded. Modern hi-tech command, control, and communication hubs and networks had to be established. Massive stockpiles of equipment had to be built up, along with hospitals for the anticipated casualties (estimated by some planners to be 1,000 per day). Each of the 8 US Divisions in Saudi Arabia (six US Army, two US Marines) required 1.6m litres (345,000 gallons) of diesel and 230,000 litres (50,000 gallons) of aviation fuel every single day. While the Saudis were able to provide a significant amount, much of the fuel the Coalition needed still had to be imported.

The US Miliary Airlift Command (MAC) began to fly troops and supplies to Saudi Arabia, Bahrain, and Qatar. The MAC were able to provide nearly 400 heavy lift aircraft to the task, but even with the support of Coalition military partners a significant number of contracted civil aircraft were also needed. Seven ports around the Saudi Arabian coast were given over to Coalition use; from ad-Damman alone a road convoy would leave every 15 minutes, and from just that one port 28,000 containers of equipment, 126,000 vehicles, 1,500 helicopters, and 360,000 tons

**"THE IRAQI ARMED FORCES WERE CONSIDERABLE IN SIZE AND HIGHLY EXPERIENCED FROM THEIR RECENT WAR WITH IRAN"**

*British Challenger tanks exercise in the desert. The UK provided the second largest tank contingent in the Coalition*

# PROTECTING SAUDI ARABIA

*An A4 Skyhawk of the Free Kuwaiti Forces in Saudi Arabia. Holding Saudi Arabia was crucial to stopping Iraq and liberating Kuwait*

The Iraqi invasion of Kuwait opened the possibility that Saddam Hussein's forces would continue to advance south into Saudi Arabia, whose armed forces were less than a tenth the size of Iraq's. The invasion had been prompted by Kuwait's oilfields and Iraq's debts, and although Saudi Arabia had supported Iraq during their recent war with Iran, this had led to Iraq building up considerable debts to the Saudis. Occupying Saudi Arabia would wipe out those debts while also giving Saddam Hussein control of the majority of the world's oil reserves. Taking control of Mecca and Medina would also assist in Hussein's self-appointed role as guardian of the Islamic world, and he repeatedly attacked Saudi Arabia as unworthy of these holy sites in his propaganda.

After a period of uncertainly, it became clear by mid-September 1990 that the Iraqis had moved to a defensive posture in Kuwait and now invasion was imminent. However, on 29 January 1991 a limited attack was made into the oilfields around the coastal city of Khafji. Three Iraqi divisions (which had already suffered during the Coalition air campaign) crossed the border, and three days of fighting saw them repulsed by US Marines, Saudi forces, and a battalion of Qatari tanks.

*President George HW Bush discusses Operation Desert Shield with his military advisers on 15 January 1991*

*Operation Desert Shield was a massive logistical undertaking, needing nearly 1m personnel and the equipment to support them*

*Qatari, American, and Canadian aircraft operate together during Operation Desert Shield*

of ammunition were transported to the forces gathering in northern Saudi Arabia.

Once in theatre, troops and equipment had to be adapted for desert use. Little of the equipment in use with the Western armies had been designed for use in the hot, dry deserts. Parts expanded or contracted in the heat, causing mechanical failure, and a steady stream of urgent requirements went out to industry and stop-gap measures were improvised. The stocks of equipment for such warfare, including desert camouflage uniforms, were lacking and had to be rapidly ordered and produced. The personnel and their equipment had been trained and optimised for the plains of Germany, or for various specialist units – the snows of Scandinavia or the jungles of South America. Troops had to be retrained in desert survival, and acclimatised to the

new conditions. Personnel speaking dozens of languages and trained in a wide range of different doctrines had to be melded into a coherent whole. While the NATO forces who had exercised and worked together before had a certain level of interoperability, even they had to standardise radio equipment and procedures as well as many other operational aspects. All of these processes took time, and it is remarkable that such extensive and varied forces were prepared for combat in such a short time.

There were also cultural issues to be navigated. Saudi Arabia is a very conservative country, with a strong Islamic identity. The influx of hundreds of thousands of secular or Christian troops, including women, was a culture-shock on both sides, and various tricky issues had to be carefully settled to prevent

either side from taking offence and upsetting Coalition troop relations.

The political aspects of the Coalition also needed careful handling, as a broad range of militaries, some of them with existing levels of friction or hostility between them, began to come together. UN Security Council support for the operation assisted greatly, although both the Soviet Union and China remained neutral.

Britain was a significant partner, able to bring over 53,000 personnel in their largest military deployment since the Korean War. The 1st (UK) Armoured Division and significant air assets were sent, while the Royal Navy made a significant contribution to the forces in the Persian Gulf, especially in the provision of modern minesweepers. France contributed a light division, although dissent over the campaign at home (France had enjoyed close

*Marine Attack Squadron 513 of the US Marine Corps fly their AV-AB Harrier II ground-attack aircraft in formation during Desert Shield*

*US 1st Battalion, 325th Airborne Infantry Regiment in a live-fire exercise with the Saudi Arabian National Guard during Desert Shield*

*Members of the US 11th Air Defense Brigade in 1992*

*Egyptian troops arrive in Saudi Arabia. The Arab world was divided in its response to the war, but several Arab countries sent significant numbers of troops*

ties with Iraq before the war) led to close political supervision by Paris. The Germans were preoccupied by reunification, but were able to provide significant funds, as did the Kuwaiti government in exile, while the Japanese were forbidden to send troops overseas by their constitution and sent money instead. Australia, New Zealand, Canada, Argentina, Belgium, Denmark, Greece, Italy, the Netherlands, Norway, Portugal, and Spain all provided small forces, generally air and naval forces, although some also sent troops. South Korea, Singapore, the then Czechoslovakia, Hungary, Sweden, Romania, the Philippines, Bangladesh, Poland, Niger, Senegal, and Sierra Leone all provided medical units. Turkey provided aircraft, and allowed other Coalition forces to use Turkish air bases on Iraq's northern border.

More difficult to rally were the Arab countries. Many Muslims objected to the presence of large numbers of non-Muslim troops in Saudi Arabia, or saw the conflict as an Arab problem to be settled within the framework of the Arab League, or (as the dispute was largely over oil production) the Organisation of Petroleum Exporting Countries (OPEC). Saddam actively attempted to exploit these divisions, ramping up his anti-Israeli propaganda and hoping to provoke the Israelis into direct action against Iraq.

Equally, the Western powers worked hard to keep Israel neutral, even housing defensive missile systems in Israel to defend the country. The direct entry of Israel into the conflict would be sure to alienate the Arab world, at best leading to widespread neutrality and at worst bringing other countries to Iraq's

aid on the battlefield. Qatar, Bahrain, the United Arab Emirates, and of course Saudi Arabia were all close neighbours of Iraq and saw their own security on the line, and provided troops, bases, and finances to the Coalition. Egypt, Morocco, and Syria also saw Iraq as a threat and provided large numbers of troops, but Jordan, Algeria, Tunisia, Mauritania, and Iran all politically supported Iraq, although stopped short of providing any military forces.

On 15 January 1991 the UN deadline for the evacuation of Kuwait passed, and at 0300 local time on 17 January one of the most effective air campaigns in history began as Coalition aircraft launched the first of over 100,000 sorties against the Iraqi forces. Operation Desert Shield had become Operation Desert Storm.

# TORNADO GR.1

## Desert Storm was the combat debut for the venerable Tornado GR.1

**WORDS:** STUART HADAWAY

A 1960s design that first flew in 1974 and entered RAF service in 1982, the Tornado proved to be one of the most versatile and longest-serving RAF jets. Created by a tri-national consortium which included Germany and Italy, the type was sold to Saudi Arabia as well, who also operated it during Operation Desert Storm. The distinctive swing-wing design was optimised for low-level high-speed interdiction, and the RAF crews had trained to launch night attacks on Soviet airfields and infrastructure over Germany for NATO. This role translated directly into the Coalition air campaign, and the Tornado's first ever combat sorties were spent attacking Iraqi airfields. Even with extensive training and experience, these operations were a risky business. Five Tornados were lost at low-level during the opening days of the war, and a sixth after their later switch to medium-level operations (three more were lost in accidents). After the successful suppression of the Iraqi air force, some GR.1s switched to medium-level operations, using laser-guided bombs. Usually operating with Blackburn Buccaneers carrying the designator pods, the Tornados continued to launch attacks on Iraqi infrastructure, especially bridges, and logistics centres. The combination obtained levels of precision previously unheard of in RAF operations.

The GR1a reconnaissance variant continued to fly at low levels throughout the war, gathering intelligence on potential targets. The end of Operation Desert Storm in February 1991 was followed immediately by a move to enforce no-fly zones, and from there the Tornado conducted a further 29 years of continuous operations over Iraq.

### DESERT PINK
All of the RAF's strike aircraft received a distinctive 'desert pink' camouflage scheme, some before being deployed but others after reaching theatre.

### IMPRESSIVE RADAR
GR.1s had two ground-mapping and terrain-following radars in their nose, allowing them to operate at low-level and high-speed at night.

### NAUGHTY NOSE ART
The Tornado squadrons adopted some rather risqué nose art while deployed on Desert Storm, which disappeared very quickly on their return to the UK.

*Tornado GR.1 from No. 14 Squadron RAF on patrol, 1991.*

## "EVEN WITH EXTENSIVE TRAINING AND EXPERIENCE, THESE OPERATIONS WERE A RISKY BUSINESS"

*Above: Tornado GR.1s being prepared for flight at King Faisal Airbase, Tabuk, Saudi Arabia.*

## PANAVIA TORNADO GR.1

| COMMISSIONED | 1968 |
|---|---|
| ORIGIN | ANGLO-GERMAN-ITALIAN |
| LENGTH | 16.72M (54FT 10IN) |
| WINGSPAN | 13.91M (45FT 8IN) |
| ENGINE | 2 X TURBO-UNION RB199 TURBOFANS WITH 40.5KN THRUST (73KN ON AFTERBURNER) |
| CREW | 2 |
| PRIMARY WEAPON | UP TO 8,620KG (19,000LB) OF AIR-DROPPED ORDNANCE |
| SECONDARY WEAPON | 2 X 27MM MAUSER CANNON |

**MOVABLE TAILERONS**
The Tornado's tailplanes were technically tailerons, with the whole plane able to swivel to improve control and responsiveness.

**HEAVY PUNCH**
With two pylons under each wing and three long pylons, each capable of carrying multiple munitions, under the fuselage, the Tornado could carry a heavy and versatile load.

*The four types of RAF aircraft used in the Gulf War, left to right: Tornado F3, Buccaneer BAe 1, Sepecat Jaguar GR1, Tornado GR1*

Images: Getty Images, Alamy

## ARMAMENT

In the opening nights of Desert Storm, RAF Tornados focused their attacks on Iraqi airfields with JP233 airfield denial weapons, which spread a mix of nearly 500 bomblets and mines over a wide area to break up airfield surfaces. Freefall bombs weighing 1,000lb (450kg) were also used. After taking heavy losses on low-level operations, and discovering that the Iraq air defences had been suitably reduced, the GR1s changed to mid-level (over 20,000ft) operations delivering both 'iron' and laser-guided bombs (usually designated by RAF Buccaneers) to attack targets day and night. GR1s also used Air-Launched Anti-Radiation Missiles (ALARMs) to attack Iraqi radar sites.

*Left: Armourers secure a 1,000lb bomb onto a GR1*

*Below: Two GR1s armed with laser-guided bombs wait to take off; rearmost is a Buccaneer carrying its laser designator*

*Bottom: A Tornado GR1 at Tabuk, showing the nose-mounted Mauser cannon and BL755 cluster bombs under the fuselage (although these bombs were never dropped in anger)*

# DESIGN

Known affectionately by the RAF as 'Tonka' due to its blocky and toy-like construction, or 'The Fin' because of its large tail, the Tornado was a design marvel. The use of variable-geometry swing wings, with a range of 25-67 degrees, allowed the wing to be adjusted to the best configurations for high-speed infiltration of enemy defences, or lower speed and longer-ranged loitering. It also gave the aircraft excellent low-speed handling characteristics. The long nose housed two different air-to-ground radar systems, while much of the rear fuselage was taken up by the two engines. The GR1a reconnaissance version had a imaging suite in the nose in place of the GR1's cannon.

# ENGINE

The Tornado used two Turbo-Union RB199 afterburning engines with a three-stage turbofan, with a thrust weighting of 40.5kN, or 73kN while on afterburner. This almost doubling of the thrust on afterburner (pushing the aircraft towards Mach 2) was rare for any engine, but was necessary to cope with the different flight profiles enabled by the variable-geometry wing. Initially developed by Rolls-Royce, the RB199 was taken on by Turbo-Union, a tri-national company created specifically to produce this engine. It had variable intake ramps and, unusually for a fighter, had thrust reversers for use on landing.

*A GR.1 in a hardened aircraft shelter at Tabuk*

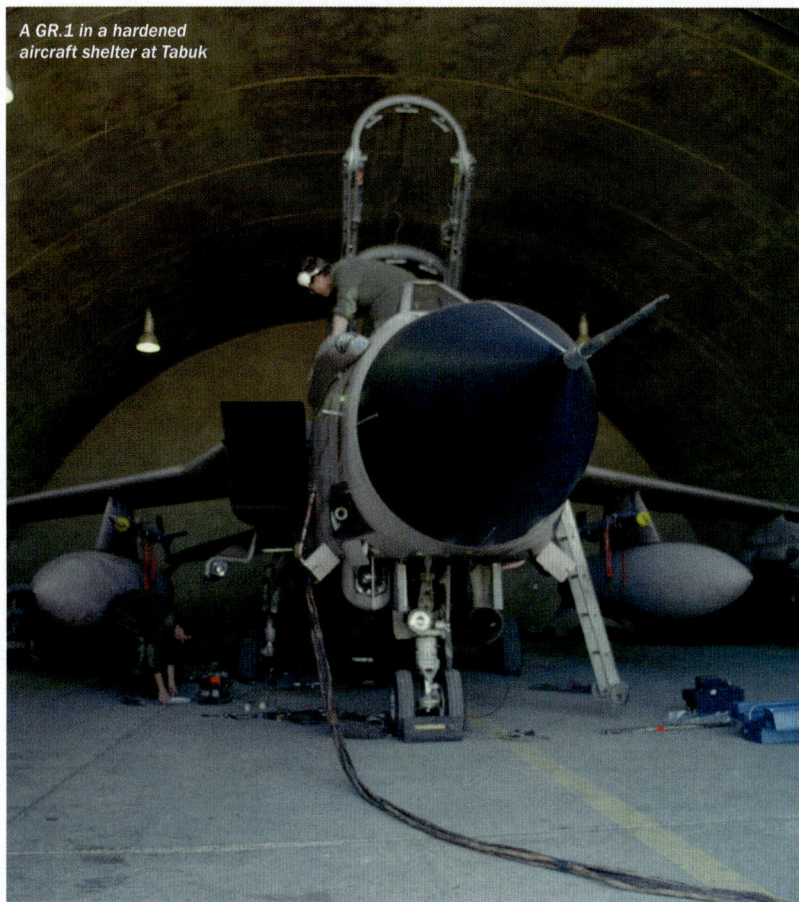

**Left:** *Exhausts of a Tornado's RB-199s, showing the afterburner mechanism within*

*The sturdy construction of the Tornado belies its speed and manoeuvrability*

Images: Getty Images, Alamy

41

# SERVICE HISTORY

The first Tornados deployed to the Gulf were F3 Air Defence Variants, rushing to Saudi Arabia within a week of the invasion of Kuwait. GR1 and GR1a types followed, arriving from 26 August 1990 at Muharraq in Bahrain and Tabuk and Dhahran in Saudi Arabia, spread on a line 870 miles (1,400km) long. Training immediately began so pilots could adapt to the desert conditions. When the air campaign began in the early hours of 17 January 1991 they adopted the role that they had trained for over Germany, making low-level night raids against enemy logistics and infrastructure. Their first targets were Iraqi airfields, making sure that the already-degraded Iraqi air force could not interfere with the coalition air strikes. From 21 January, operations became more varied as daylight medium-level operations started, with laser-guided bombs to target airfields, bridges, supply dumps and power stations; ALARMs were used to target radar sites. The flights, whether training or operational, were dangerous, and nine Tornado GR1s were lost during Operations Desert Shield and Desert Storm, with seven crewmen killed and seven captured. The prisoners of war faced torture by the Iraqis before their eventual release. However, the Tornados had provided the coalition with crucial and highly effective capabilities.

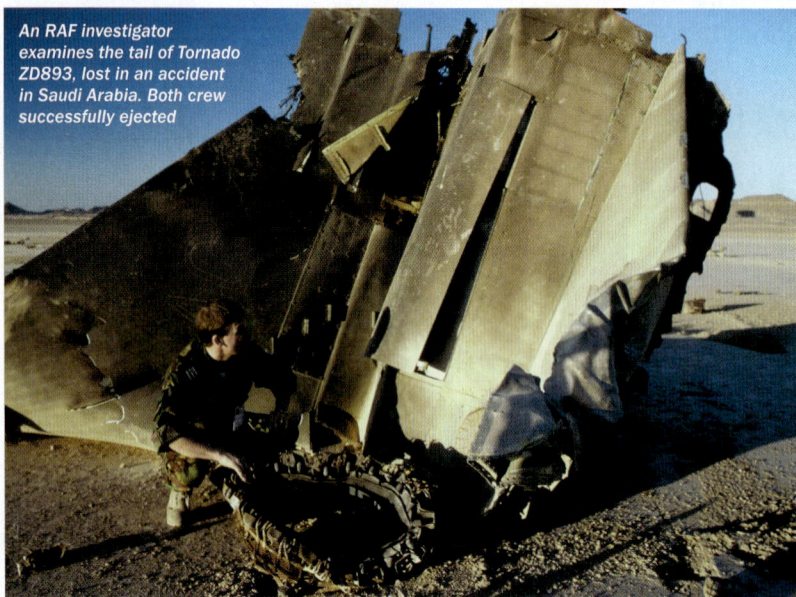

An RAF investigator examines the tail of Tornado ZD893, lost in an accident in Saudi Arabia. Both crew successfully ejected

*Initially, the GR.1s operated only at night*

"THE FIRST TORNADOS DEPLOYED TO THE GULF WERE F3 AIR DEFENCE VARIANTS, RUSHING TO SAUDI ARABIA WITHIN A WEEK OF THE INVASION OF KUWAIT"

## COCKPIT

The Tornado crew sat in a tandem cockpit, with the pilot in the front and the Weapons System Officer (WSO) in the rear. The WSO was responsible for navigation, weapons, and counter-measures, and could get extremely busy during the low-level attack runs over heavily defended targets that the Tornado was designed for. Ground-imaging and terrain-following radars assist with the low-flying. The controls and avionics included a significant amount of mechanical redundancy due to the Tornados potential role as a tactical nuclear bomber, so that the aircraft would remain effective even after being caught in the resulting electro-magnetic pulse.

# TORNADO IN A STORM

On the first day of the Coalition offensive, Flight Lieutenant John Nichol was shot down while attacking an Iraqi air base. Here he shares his memories of the war, what it was like ejecting over the desert, and his time as a POW

**WORDS: TIM WILLIAMSON**

*Nichol with John Peters pictured before their first flight together since being shot down in 1991*

*An abandoned Soviet-made anti-air-artillery piece, used to defend an Iraqi airbase*

### What do you remember about the buildup to Operation Desert Storm?

**John Nichol:** When it all started back in August 1990 [with] the invasion of Kuwait… It was a lightning bolt out of the blue…The Tornado Force had never been used in anger and I think many of us didn't think it ever would [be]. Because it was a tactical Nuclear Strike Force it was designed for the Cold War stopping the Soviets coming over what was then the East German border. So it was bloody exciting – the notion of doing the job for real. We were like firefighters who'd never been to a blaze, and suddenly somebody had lit a bloody great fire.

Different parts of the Tornado Force were sent out at different times and so training started, but the first people went out within a few hours and then we thought: "We're not prepared. We're gonna die…" By the time we got there in December it was enormous… It was something like a million troops in the desert ready to go. We landed in Bahrain and I've never seen anything like it. There were hundreds of tactical aircraft tankers and when you flew over any of the Saudi airfields, they were just rammed. If you flew over the desert you would look down on these encampments of hundreds of thousands of troops. The scale was enormous.

### What sort of preparations and training did you take part in?

**John Nichol:** We were in intense training during the summer; air-to-air refuelling, tactical profiles, and then when we got out to the desert…. The Tornado was a low-level tactical force, so low-level night flying… eight aircraft in formation at night, no lights, practising blind attacks. That training buildup was intense, but very few of us thought we would ever start the war, right up until probably two or three days before. But even then I personally thought the politicians would sort this out, and then suddenly we were going and I really remember that moment.

It would have been 16 January because my formation started its shift at about 11pm or 10pm and I could hear my squadron singing the squadron song that was sung before the final attack of every training exercise, which was the mass nuclear launch – the end of the world, you sang the song.

I went in and I could hear this song… and I said to my pilot JP: "We're going." I still get shivers now thinking about that. That was an astonishing moment of personal reality.

### What did you know about your target and your role in the opening day of the war?

**John Nichol:** Our boss and the guy who was planning the operations knew what the targets were going to be for the first three days, but we absolutely did not know. So the first night attack was revealed to the crews a few hours before, and then our target was revealed that night. Without releasing it, we'd been practising an almost identical profile for the previous week… So [we were told]: "Here's your target, it is on the border, you're gonna go along here to refuel, drop down across the border, go this way you come out [and then] the tanker will meet you here and then you'll come home." The last bit didn't happen.

**Q *You were the second sortie of your squadron to attack. Did you get any sense of what to expect at all?***

*John Nichol:* We were listening on the military radio. Tallil air base was attacked at 2am so they were heading home at about 3am or 4am, and we were listening to it on the radio while we were doing our planning ... We heard them checking in ready to come back to the airfield, and none of us believed that they would all come home.

We thought a number of aircraft would be shot down because it was so dangerous and we were flying over the most heavily defended targets apart from Baghdad itself, at low level... so when we heard all eight jets from our squadron coming home, I was astonished that everybody had come out unscathed. It was definitely not what I'd expected.

As we were walking out to get into our aircraft to go, which was four in the morning so the sun was coming up [and] my best mate was walking back in... that was the last time I saw them for seven weeks.

**How well prepared were you for Anti-Aircraft Artillery fire?**

*John Nichol:* It had never been really spoken about. All of our defences were against heat-seeking missiles from the Iraqi Air Force – their fighters, interceptors, their tactics – [as well as] ground-to-air missiles, the big ones that defended the major bases like SAM 3 or SAM 6. We had electronic warfare pods, we had chaff, we had flares... so all of our preparations were against that kind of threat, because you can't do anything about Triple-A (Anti-Aircraft Artillery). But nobody knew the effect it would have on you.

Somebody had said that the Triple-A coming up was astonishing... But it was just something in the background as we flew in...you could certainly see the odd puff of smoke as a shell exploded, but you have no concept that behind every little puff of smoke there's another 10,000 exploding bullets going off.

**What can you recall about being shot down?**

*John Nichol:* It was somebody on the ground – there were Iraqi emplacements everywhere. As we would have if we were there, we would have shoulder-held surface-to-air missiles... and it was one of those.

After the war they [recovered] bits of the wreckage, and you can see holes in the Sidewinder missile where the shrapnel from the missile exploded and went through. So it was somebody on the ground, [with a] heat-seeking missile from the rear-right quarter, because we never saw it coming...If we'd seen it coming clearly we could have deployed flares in the effort to evade it. Now there's automatic devices that can give missile approach warnings that can do that kind of thing. We didn't have any of that.

This was 1991 in a tornado GR1, which is the first Mark of tornado. So... it's 1960s-70s technology. It was really old fashioned [but] still an incredibly capable aircraft.

**What do you remember about ejecting over the desert?**

*John Nichol:* Unlike other people, we had a few minutes to prepare... We had maybe 30 seconds after being hit to try to see if we were going to be able to get home, but the aircraft was on fire.... JP pulled up, I think we may have been at something like 200 feet, and we had slowed down, so we weren't at high speed.

Pulling the [ejector] handle I remember a click. Then I could just see out of the seat a jet of flame as the rockets ignited from between my legs. You don't black out, but your eyes are obviously forced shut. There's a very quick tumbling sensation and then a "snap" as the parachute opens. It's near instantaneous: a sensation of flame, sensation of tumbling, a crack and then silence...then you're in a parachute. My first ever parachute jump... with the Iraqi desert beneath me.

*Below: Parts of Nichol's crashed Tornado, later recovered, which included a Sidewinder missile (with shrapnel and 23mm holes), RB199 engine, front nose probe and weapon pylon*

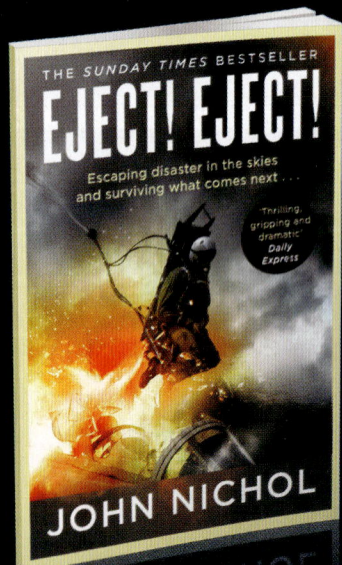

THE SUNDAY TIMES BESTSELLER

# EJECT! EJECT!

Escaping disaster in the skies and surviving what comes next...

*Thrilling, gripping and dramatic' Daily Express*

JOHN NICHOL

# EJECT! EJECT!

## ESCAPING DISASTER IN THE SKIES AND SURVIVING WHAT COMES NEXT

The updated paperback of John Nichol's bestselling history of ejection seats, the pioneers who invented them and the incredible stories of the aviators whose lives they saved, is available now from Simon and Schuster

Inset: Tornado training in the desert at low-level, armed with the JP233 anti-runway weapon system

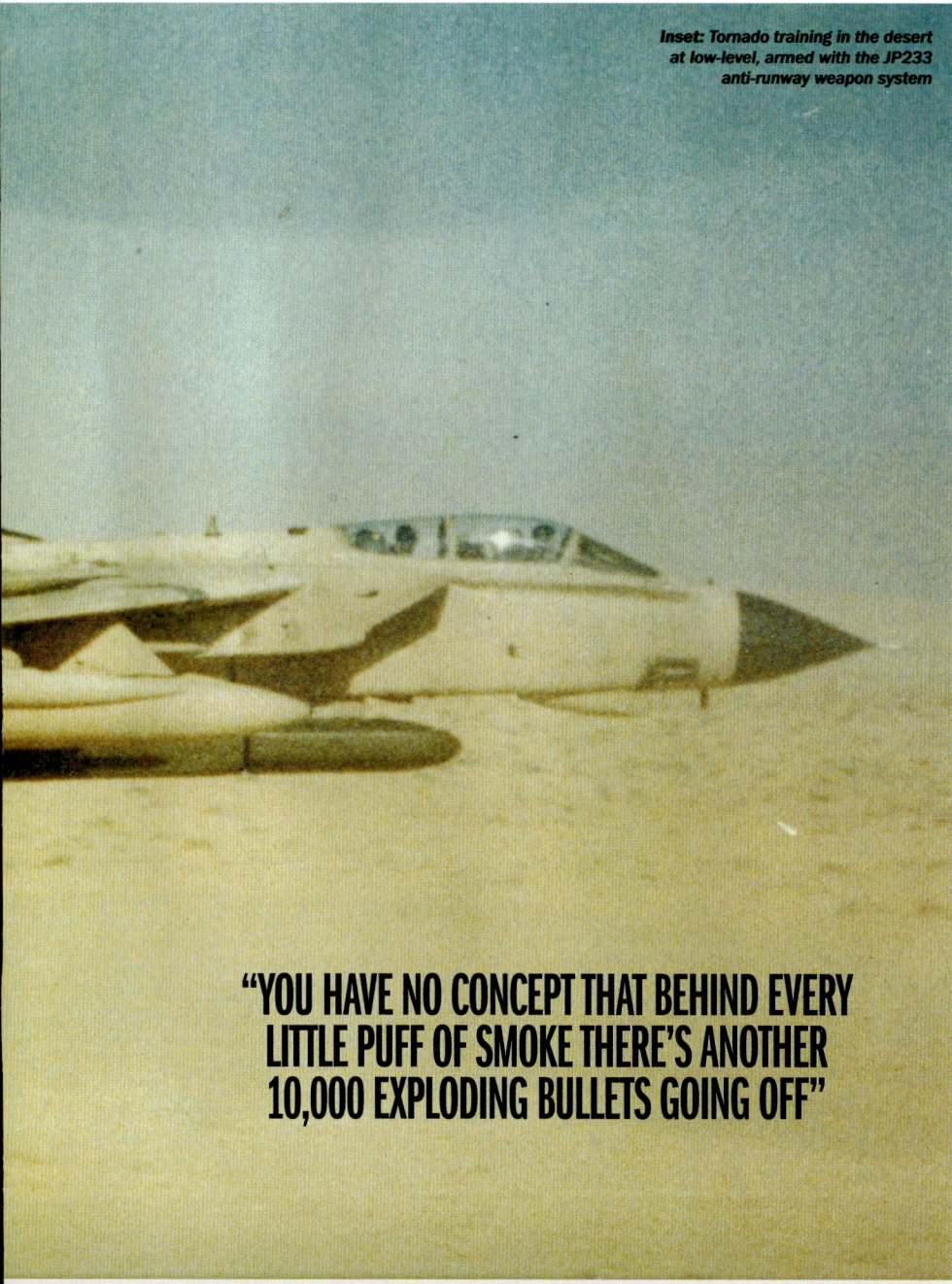

# PRISONER IN BAGHDAD

AFTER BEING CAPTURED, NICHOL ENDURED OVER SEVEN WEEKS OF CAPTIVITY, DURING WHICH HE WAS BEATEN, TORTURED AND PARADED ON TELEVISION BY THE IRAQIS

Upon landing in their ejector seats, Nichol realised how unprepared he was to survive in the desert, let alone evade the enemy. "There'd been a bit of a classroom lecture on desert survival… but almost nothing," he recalls. "There was no training about what we now refer to as conduct after capture. That changed completely because of our experiences."

When the Iraqis found him, Nichol feared the worst. "I certainly thought I'd be murdered, or tortured to death. We had no concept about the reality of what was going to happen." Now a prisoner of war, Nichol was isolated, interrogated and tortured for days, before being paraded on Iraqi television.

During his imprisonment, Nichol was cut off from the outside world. "Maybe for three or four weeks… I never saw or heard another person, because you're behind a three-inch thick steel door in a concrete [room] with three-feet thick walls," he recalls. "Obviously the one thing that you did know is that bombing was going on because you could hear it every night and… depending on where you were, you were being bombed."

On 28 February, gunfire and celebrations could be heard outside the prison. "The cacophony of yelling and cheering and the guns firing into the air was terrifying because you didn't know what was going on. The Iraqi media had announced that they had won."

On 5 May, Nichol and his comrades finally received the news they had been waiting for: "An Iraqi came into the cell and said: "The war's over, you can go home.""

> "YOU HAVE NO CONCEPT THAT BEHIND EVERY LITTLE PUFF OF SMOKE THERE'S ANOTHER 10,000 EXPLODING BULLETS GOING OFF"

# SCUD

## BALLISTIC MISSILES

### Iraq's long-reach terror weapon

**WORDS:** STUART HADAWAY

Scud ballistic missiles were perhaps the most feared weapon in Saddam Hussein's arsenal in 1991. 'Scud' became a generic term for the 1961-designed R-17 Short-Range Ballistic Missile (NATO reporting name: Scud-B) and the locally produced al-Husayn variant. In order to reach strategic targets in Iran during the Iran-Iraq War (1980-88), the Iraqis took the Scud-B, lightened the warhead to 500kg (1,102lb) and increased the propellent chamber to double the range, although at the cost of accuracy. The resulting al-Husayn was specifically designed with a modified thruster profile to land a warhead anywhere within 650km (400 miles) of Iraq's borders in just 8 minutes flight time; a radius that included Riyadh, Bahrain, Qatar, and Tel Aviv.

Equipped with conventional, chemical, or biological warheads, Scud missiles became a fixation for the Coalition forces.

Highly mobile, easy to hide in pre-prepared positions or spoof with carefully prepared decoys, and operating in a huge desert, locating and attempting to disable these elusive weapons would consume significant amounts of resources. Hundreds of Coalition aircraft sorties and numerous Special Forces teams would scour Iraq's western desert for Scud launchers with remarkably little success, with very few recorded attacks and no confirmed destructions of launchers.

Neither the Scuds or al-Husayns were particularly accurate, and while 93 were launched at targets in Saudi Arabia, Israel, and Bahrain, they generally met with little physical success. Their main achievement was psychological and in the propaganda war, boosting Iraqi morale while remaining a constant concern for the Coalition at all levels.

### POTENT WARHEAD
The al-Husayn's warhead was relatively small but potent, and in particular the threat of chemical or biological ordnance was taken extremely seriously.

### AREA WEAPON
The al-Husayn was accurate at best to a 1,000-metre radius, although with chemical weapons pinpoint accuracy was not necessary.

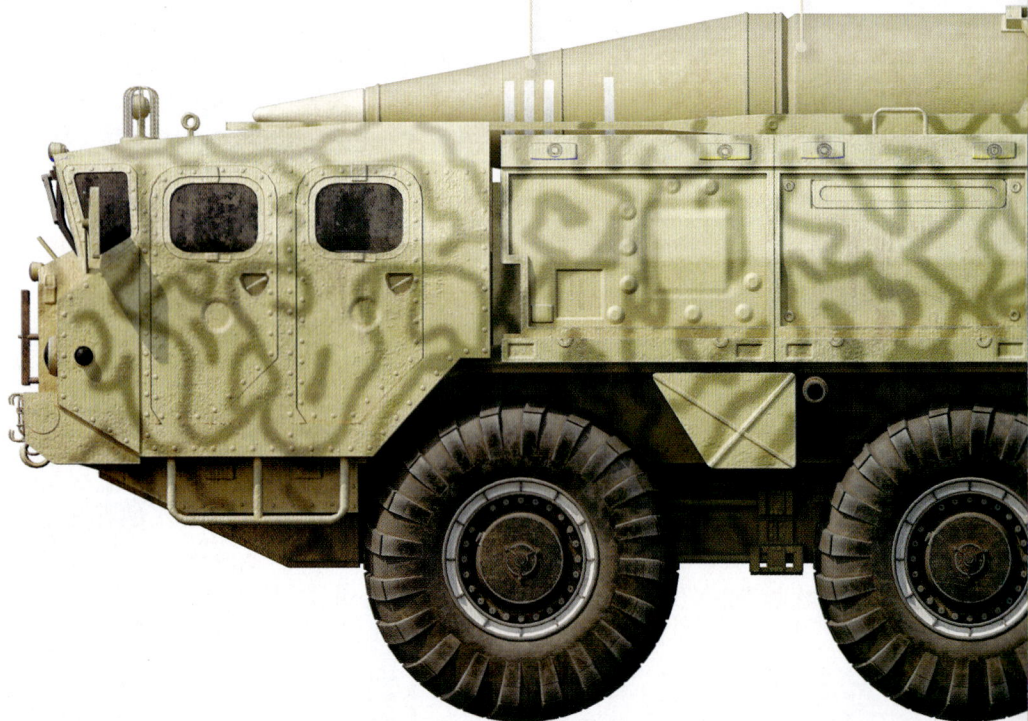

# AL-HUSAYN SHORT RANGE BALLISTIC MISSILE

| COMMISSIONED | 1987 |
|---|---|
| ORIGIN | IRAQI |
| LENGTH | 12.46M (41.5FT) |
| RANGE | 650KM (400 MILES) |
| ENGINE | LIQUID PROPELLED ROCKET MOTOR |
| CREW | 8 |
| PRIMARY WEAPON | 500KG (1,102LB) WARHEAD |

## "THE AL-HUSAYN WAS DESIGNED TO LAND A WARHEAD ANYWHERE WITHIN 400 MILES OF IRAQ'S BORDERS IN JUST 8 MINUTES"

### NARROW DIAMETER
The missile was only 0.88m in diameter and structurally weak. Missiles frequently broke up in flight, confusing Coalition counter-measures.

### LOW PROFILE
The narrowness of the rocket and low profile of the launchers meant they were hard to detect and easy to spoof in decoy sites.

### SIMPLE BUT EFFECTIVE
The Scud had a simple, mechanically reliable single-chambered engine with anti-oscillation baffles.

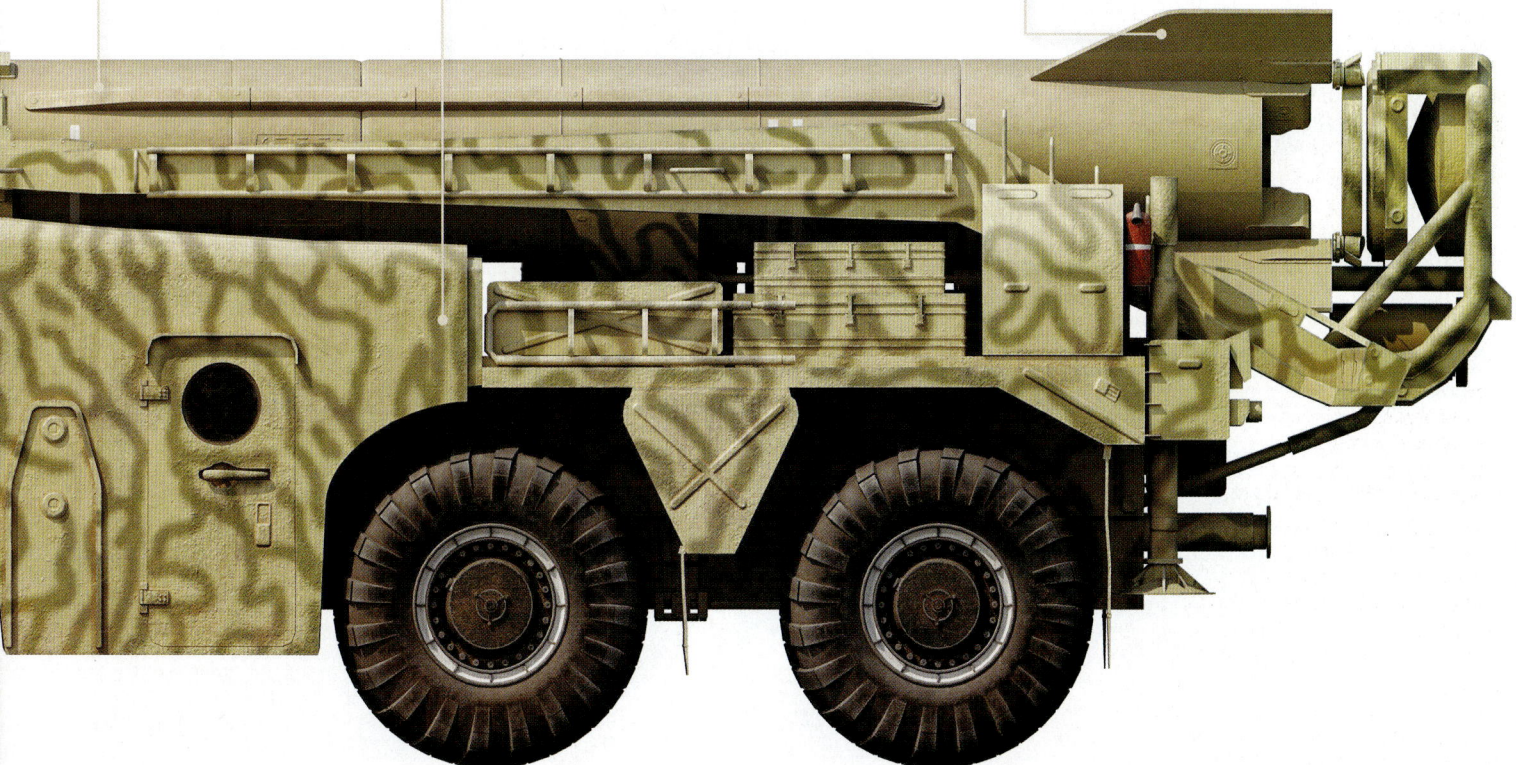

*Illustration: Nicholas Forder. Image: Alamy*

# WARHEAD

The original Scud-B could carry a 985kg (2,172lb) warhead, which could consist of conventional, nuclear, biological, or chemical materials. The al-Husayn was designed around a warhead capable of only half that weight, as a major part of the scheme to increase its range to hit Iranian cities. In 1990-91, the increased range was a major factor in the threat that these missiles posed, as was Saddam Hussein's known stockpiles of chemical weapons, estimated at between 2,000 and 4,000 tons of mustard gas, Sarin, and Tabun. Even in reduced warheads, such materials would wreak havoc in major population centres or troop concentrations.

*Inset, Right: Parts of Scud missiles, including two warheads (left), from later strikes on display in Israel*

*Below: Devastation caused in Tel Aviv by a Scud missile*

*A camouflaged Scud launch site photographed by a F-14A Tomcat, the dark patches showing Coalition bomb craters.*

# "IN THE GULF WAR THE INCREASED RANGE WAS A MAJOR FACTOR IN THE THREAT THAT THESE MISSILES POSED"

## ENGINE

The al-Husayn ballistic missile used a simple rocket motor engine, burning a mixture of 22 per cent kerosene and 78 per cent nitric acid oxidiser to produce thrust. The al-Husayn differed from the Scud-B by having a larger fuel tank, and a much higher speed. The 4500kg (9921lb) of fuel would burn in the first 50km (31 miles) of the rocket's flight (which peaked at 151 km (94 miles) of altitude), leaving the missile to descend towards its target at speeds in excess of Mach 7 (the Scud-B would reach Mach 5).

## DESIGN

The R-17 'Scud B' Short Range Ballistic Missile was a simple but potent design: a long tube 0.88m (2ft 11in) in diameter had a single liquid fuelled rocket at one end and a versatile warhead on the top. It had a range of 300km (190 miles). The al-Husayn development was the same basic design, but was longer, with a smaller warhead, and a larger fuel tank. This changed the centre of gravity and led to structural problems, with many rockets breaking up as they reached the apogee of their flights, something which confused Coalition radar and interfered with anti-ballistic missile systems.

**Left:** *An Iraqi missile awaiting destruction outside Baghdad after the Gulf War*

**Below:** *The rear section of a shot-down Iraqi Scud in 1991, showing it's long, narrow construction*

*Images: Alamy, Getty Images*

# LAUNCH VEHICLE

Scud missiles could be launched from fixed sites, although the obvious likelihood of these being targeted led to most being used from mobile launchers, called Transporter Erector Launchers (TELs). The Scud-B used the Soviet MA2-543 heavy wheeled transporter, and initially the al-Husayn used locally produced al-Nida and (possibly) al-Waleed launchers. However, these lacked reliability and many MA2-543s were modified for the longer al-Husayns. TEL launch sequences were officially 90 minutes, but operationally this was often cut to 30 minutes, with the TELs then rapidly moving into cover. This gave Coalition forces frustratingly fleeting targets, and very few were engaged or destroyed.

*A captured Iraqi TEL, now on display in the US*

*Inside the crew compartment of an Iraqi Scud TEL*

# SERVICE HISTORY

In 1990, the Scud-B and al-Husayn ballistic missile systems were used by the 223, 224 and 225 Missile Brigades. Mostly based in Iraq's massive 75,000 square kilometre (29,000 square mile) western desert, they utilised fixed and mobile sites. Numerous decoy sites were established, as well as carefully camouflaged hiding places for TELs between launches.

The Iraqi missile campaign started on 18 January 1991, 48 hours after the Coalition air operations began. Until the end of February, approximately 93 missiles were launched, including 46 towards Saudi Arabia and 42 towards Israel. Results were generally poor. The force's mobility, while improving survivability, decreased accuracy as temporary sites were used and launches were rushed. While this allowed the TELs to almost entirely avoid the Coalition aircraft (15% of sorties from 16-30 January 1991) and Special Forces patrols (including the infamous SAS Bravo Two Zero) that sought them, few rockets reached their intended targets. The US Patriot anti-ballistic missile system was lauded at the time, but there were actually few successful interceptions, and most Scuds actually broke up in flight or landed in open desert.

The most successful missile came late in the campaign, on 25 February 1991, when it hit a US base at Dhahran, Saudi Arabia, killing 28 service personnel and wounding over 100.

*Right: British troops in chemical and biological warfare suits wait for the all-clear after a Scud attack, Saudi Arabia, February 1991*

"TEL LAUNCH SEQUENCES WERE OFTEN CUT TO 30 MINUTES. THIS GAVE COALITION FORCES FRUSTRATINGLY FLEETING TARGETS"

# SCUD BUSTERS

Before the Coalition's ground offensive to liberate Kuwait commenced, Special Forces conducted dangerous missile-hunting missions inside Iraq

Aside from the dangers posed by Saddam Hussein's chemical weapons stockpiles, a particular threat faced by the Coalition's ground troops was his considerable arsenal of tactical ballistic missiles. These had successfully rained death and destruction down on Iran's cities during the bloody eight-year long Iran-Iraq War.

Coalition commanders were well aware of the threat posed by these missiles. As the Soviet-designed Scud was inaccurate, it was not really a viable military weapon, so Saddam once again resorted to using it as a terror weapon against civilian targets. During the Coalition build-up for Desert Storm/Desert Sabre, he harassed Saudi Arabia and Israel with repeated rocket and Scud missile attacks.

Saddam first fired his Soviet-made Scud B missiles at Iran in 1982; this culminated six years later in the 'War of the Cities' in which both sides fired hundreds of missiles at each other. The enormity of this should not be underestimated by anyone; Saddam's bombardment in 1988 caused 8,000 Iranian casualties and drove out a quarter of Tehran's population. A decade later Iran targeted Iranian opposition forces with missiles who were being sheltered by Saddam.

Saddam, by the time of the invasion of Kuwait, still had stocks of Scud B missiles plus his indigenously modified variants known as the Al-Abbas, Al-Hussien and Al-Hijarah. In the build-up to war 46 Scuds were fired at Saudi Arabia and another 40 at Israel. One particular strike against a barracks at Dhahran in Saudi killed 28 members of a US Army unit.

British special operations against Iraq were the responsibility of the 22nd Special Air Service (SAS) Regiment and their naval counterparts the Special Boat Squadron (SBS). The SAS deployed from their depots at Hereford, Cyprus and Oman. However, a few SAS members were already in Kuwait with the British Military Assistance Training team advising the Kuwaiti Army at the time of Saddam's invasion. They were able to provide invaluable intelligence on the local conditions.

The SAS, using their well-honed covert tactics, roamed the Iraqi army's rear areas in their Landrover Desert Patrol Vehicles, known as 'Pink Panthers' and their Longline Light Strike Vehicles. The SBS cooperated with the US Navy SEALS, who were given responsibility for raids into the Kuwait City area. Dramatically on 7 January 1991, US and British Special Forces penetrated an Iraqi air defence missile site and made off with a Soviet manufactured radar system.

The Coalition's combined air forces launched Operation Desert Storm round the clock in mid-January 1991, targeting Saddam's missile installations, lines of communication and his command and control centres. The

American Patriot missiles were used to shoot down Iraqi Scuds

F-117A stealth fighters of the US 37th Tactical Fighter Wing played a massive role in the Coalition's devastating air war against Iraq. In particular they were tasked to attack Saddam's weapons of mass destruction and command and control facilities.

While Iraq's air defences were considerable, RAF Tornado pilot Flight Lieutenant John Peters and his colleagues were also conscious of the threat from small arms. He recalled, "Since it takes very little wit to fire a gun into the air, Saddam Hussein's threat of creating 'lead walls' – curtains of fire for us happy chappies to fly into – had to be taken seriously."

Nonetheless air superiority over Kuwait and Iraq was achieved within just 24 hours of the first air attacks. The Iraqi Air Force lost almost 50 percent of its inventory, 141 aircraft were claimed destroyed on the ground, 35 in air-to air engagements, whilst 122 fled to Iran never to be returned. The national air defence system was quickly and efficiently smashed to pieces. The first salvo of sea-launched Tomahawk Land Attack Missiles or TLAMs were fired by the cruiser USS San Jacinto on 17 January 1991, followed by the attack submarines USS Pittsburgh and USS Louisville. In total 288 TLAMs were launched against Iraqi targets.

Despite the ferocity of Desert Storm and the Coalition's massed firepower, few of Saddam's Scuds were actually destroyed. Although Special Forces and Coalition pilots claimed up to 100 launchers, this figure was never substantiated. Many of those targeted proved to be lame ducks or decoys.

> "THE F-117A STEALTH FIGHTERS OF THE US 37TH TACTICAL FIGHTER WING PLAYED A MASSIVE ROLE IN THE COALITION'S DEVASTATING AIR WAR AGAINST IRAQ"

## BRAVO TWO ZERO

### A DARING BRITISH SCUD-BUSTING MISSION WENT HORRIBLY WRONG AND BECAME THE STUFF OF LEGEND

Special Forces in support of Desert Storm were tasked with not only gathering intelligence and to vector in air strikes, but also if necessary destroy Saddam's missile launchers themselves. One of the most well-known of these was the British SAS mission call-sign 'Bravo Two Zero'. Their task was to go Scud busting but the patrol was soon compromised and most of its members captured.

This operation was subsequently made famous by team member Steven Mitchell (using the pseudonym Andy McNab) who wrote a controversial book about their daring exploits. Later books by other team members conflicted with some details of Mitchell's account, leading to accusations of fabrication. McNab went on to become a highly successful novelist of both fiction and non-fiction.

WHO DARES WINS

Coalition troops inspect the remains of an Iraqi Scud missile

The aftermath of an Iraqi Scud missile attack in Tel Aviv, Israel, 24 January 1991

# THE DEMISE OF BRAVO TWO ZERO

During the 1991 Gulf War, an SAS operation
in the Iraqi desert went terribly wrong

**WORDS:** MICHAEL E. HASKEW

The situation began to unravel from the start. They were trained to complete their missions against long odds, operating behind enemy lines. But when communications could not be established and their presence was apparently discovered, there was no real choice but to abort, exfiltrate and attempt to fight another day.

The eight-man team of B Squadron 22 SAS known as Bravo Two Zero, deployed hours earlier into the trackless Iraqi desert, then began an incredible and tragic odyssey, the circumstances of which are still debated more than 30 years later.

## Prelude to deployment

When Saddam Hussein sent the Iraqi Army into Kuwait on 2 August 1990, condemnation from the community of nations was virtually unanimous, and a coalition force from 35 countries assembled to deal with the dictator's naked aggression against his neighbour. During the build-up for Operation Desert Storm, SAS formations deployed to forward operating bases in Saudi Arabia. They brought with them expertise in the covert operations that were deemed essential to the successful prosecution of the offensive, which began on 17 January 1991, to eject the Iraqis from Kuwait.

Founded during WWII as an elite special forces unit of the British Army, the SAS had earned the reputation of a highly skilled fighting force, and more recently 22 SAS had gained notoriety with their rescue of hostages from the Iranian embassy in London in 1980.

During the opening days of Desert Storm, several apparent threats to Coalition personnel were identified, and 22 SAS were detailed to eliminate – or at least impair – the ability of the Iraqi forces to launch tactical ballistic missiles, or Scuds, which were capable of delivering high-explosive warheads against both military and civilian targets. Bravo Two Zero, one of three SAS teams with similar missions, were inserted into the Iraqi desert on the night of 22–23 January.

## Scud hunters

Detailed planning was essential to the success of the Bravo Two Zero mission, and on its face the task was daunting. The team consisted of its commander, Sergeant Steven Billy Mitchell, second-in-command Sergeant Vince David Phillips, Corporal Colin Armstrong, Lance Corporal Ian Robert 'Dinger' Pring, and Troopers Robert Consiglio, Steven 'Legs' Lane, Malcolm MacGown and Mike 'Kiwi' Coburn (a pseudonym).

Numerous aspects of the Bravo Two Zero saga have been disputed, and members of the team have even put forth different interpretations of the mission itself. According to Sergeant Mitchell, writing under the

*Above: Soldiers examine the remnants of a Scud missile during the 1991 Gulf War*

*Left: The SAS men of Bravo Two Zero pose before their ill-fated mission*

*Below: Andy McNab's bestseller, chronicling his experience with Bravo Two Zero, stirred controversy*

pseudonym Andy McNab, the objective was to seek and destroy Iraqi Scud launchers along a 155-mile stretch of the Iraqi Army's main supply route. However, Corporal Armstrong, writing as Chris Ryan, asserted that the team were to find a suitable lying-up position, gather intelligence, and monitor the movements of enemy troops and Scud launchers.

Regardless, key decisions were made that heavily influenced the outcome of the mission. Although each SAS member was assigned to carry a load of equipment and supplies

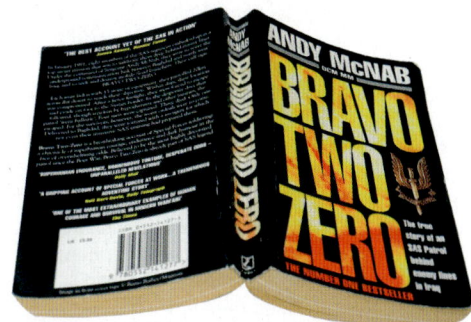

estimated to weigh at least 210 pounds, the team chose not to utilise vehicles since their numbers were few, the vehicles themselves were small, and their usefulness would be limited in an operation that was to be conducted from a fixed position.

## Mission and misstep

In the predawn darkness, Bravo Two Zero were inserted by Chinook helicopter into the desert 200 miles behind enemy lines and northwest of the Iraqi capital of Baghdad. Accounts differ as to how far the men walked that night, but temperatures were unusually cold.

"We found a perfect lying-up place," McNab (Mitchell) wrote in his 1993 bestseller, *Bravo Two Zero*. "Dead ground, out of sight and with cover from enemy fire... It was time to transmit our first Sit Rep (situation report) back to SAS base camp in Saudi, telling them where we were and what state we were in. On the patrol radio, Legs, our signaller, sent the encoded message in a single, very short burst... We waited for the acknowledgment, but none came... If the SAS base didn't hear from you, the rule was that you trekked back to the landing site and rendezvoused at a set time with a helicopter to pick up new radios."

Unknown to the team, their messages were being received at the base, but they were unable to receive any communications in return.

The following morning, an Iraqi shepherd boy stumbled across the Bravo Two Zero hiding place. McNab realised their cover was blown,

and the team began to move south towards the expected helicopter rendezvous point. He asserted in 1993 that the patrol soon met a formidable force of Iraqi troops and armoured personnel carriers, and though later investigations cast some doubt on his account, McNab wrote of a fierce firefight.

"We pulled our scarves over our faces and set out, making good progress with the Sun in our eyes until suddenly we heard the sound of more tracked vehicles. Adrenaline rushed, blood pumped. We stopped. We couldn't go forward, we couldn't go back – and we were probably no more than seconds away from contact... 'Let's do it!' I yelled... Rounds thumped into the ground, getting closer and closer to where I lay. A truck stopped 100 yards away and infantry were spilling out shouting and firing... We were now all furiously getting rounds off. One of our rockets hit a truck and there was a massive shudder of high-explosive... Mark and

## "I STARTED HALLUCINATING AND SEEING VISIONS OF MY DAUGHTER. IT WAS THAT VIVID I WAS PUTTING MY HAND OUT TO GET A HOLD OF HER AND SHE WAS TALKING TO ME"

Dinger reached one of the Iraqi APCs, found the rear doors carelessly left open and lobbed in a grenade. The occupants were killed instantly."

When the slugfest was over, scores of Iraqi soldiers lay dead on the ground; others were seriously wounded. Miraculously, none of the SAS men had been injured. When the team reassembled, McNab attempted to contact the AWACS surveillance aircraft, but his tactical distress beacon (TACBE) received no response. Further, an RAF Chinook dispatched to extricate the team at the anticipated rendezvous point was forced to turn back. McNab then decided to move northwest towards the Syrian border rather than south towards Saudi Arabia. The Syrian frontier was closer and perhaps even an alternative discussed prior to the mission. However, the deviation from the standard southern trek may well have nullified any further attempts to locate and recover the SAS team.

## Evasion, capture and death

During the night of 24 January, as McNab attempted to contact the AWACS, the eight-man group became separated. While five waited for TACBE confirmation, Phillips, MacGown and Ryan (Armstrong) continued moving towards the Syrian border. Phillips soon began to suffer the effects of hypothermia, and hours later he died of exposure to the bitter cold. Around

*Above, right: Bravo Two Zero commander Andy McNab (Sergeant Mitchell) obscures his face from a camera*

# BRAVO TWO ZERO BECOMES LEGEND

**BOOKS AND TELEVISION ADAPTATIONS HAVE BROUGHT BRAVO TWO ZERO FAME AND ADDITIONAL SCRUTINY**

In addition to McNab's (Mitchell) 1993 book, *Bravo Two Zero* and Ryan's (Armstrong) 1995 work, *The One That Got Away*, Peter Ratcliffe, the SAS Regimental Sergeant Major at the time of the operation, wrote the book *Eye Of The Storm* in 2000, a memoir that also introduces contradictory information about the abortive mission. In 2001, former SAS Trooper Michael Asher travelled to Iraq and conducted numerous interviews with witnesses while retracing the Bravo Two Zero patrol route. His book, *The Real Bravo Two Zero*, which is largely at odds with the accounts of McNab and Ryan, was published the following year. Trooper Mike 'Kiwi' Coburn also wrote a book, *Soldier Five*, published in 2004.

"I wanted to portray events as they really happened," Coburn said in reference to other available material, particularly labelling some of what McNab and Ryan wrote as fiction. "You can't have all this rubbish out there."

The Ministry of Defence failed in its attempt to suppress Coburn's book but has received all of the proceeds from its sales.

The BBC, ITV and Channel 4 have all produced documentaries based on the accounts of the SAS survivors of Bravo Two Zero and those who subsequently sought to shed light on the events.

*Below: Bravo Two Zero has been explored in books and television documentaries*

noon on 26 January, MacGown and Ryan encountered an elderly goat herder. Rather than killing the old man, they decided that MacGown would go with him and attempt to locate a vehicle while Ryan remained behind, anticipating contact with MacGown in a few hours. Ryan later reported that MacGown came upon several men with a Toyota Landcruiser, shot one individual as he ran towards it, and then gunned down another pair. Out of ammunition and unable to flee in the Toyota, he was captured. McNab's account of MacGown's skirmish differs from that of Ryan, but it is only one of many contradictions.

Meanwhile, McNab's group hijacked a taxi and drove some distance to an Iraqi checkpoint, where Lane reportedly shot one sentry while two more were killed by other members of the SAS team. Again, Ryan contradicts McNab, and further investigation years later failed to confirm the actual sequence of events. Subsequently, it is known that Consiglio was killed by hostile fire during a confrontation with local police and civilians in the early morning hours of 27 January. Lane and Pring swam the Euphrates River that morning, and Lane died of hypothermia a short time later. Coburn was wounded in the arm and ankle. In short order, the three survivors of McNab's group were taken prisoner.

*The One That Got Away author and Bravo Two Zero survivor Chris Ryan addresses a gathering*

# "I WANTED TO PORTRAY EVENTS AS THEY REALLY HAPPENED. YOU CAN'T HAVE ALL THIS RUBBISH OUT THERE"

Above: A Chinook inserted the team into the desert, but the one headed for the rendezvous point had to turn back

## Ryan's incredible journey

Ryan, however, remained at large. In fact, he began an incredible trek of approximately 180 miles to the Syrian frontier and safety, the longest such journey undertaken by an SAS trooper – or perhaps any soldier – in history. However, as with so many other aspects of the Bravo Two Zero mission, Ryan's account remains the subject of scrutiny and conjecture to this day.

During a harrowing week, Ryan maintains, he crossed the desert towards Syria. Surviving the bone-chilling cold each night, he had to find water. But when he came upon a pool and drank, his throat burned and he retched. The creek he had drawn from was downstream from an Iraqi nuclear facility and had been contaminated with a toxic substance known as 'yellowcake'.

In February 2021, he explained to Forces News, "For the last three nights I had nothing and I was walking about 40 kilometres [25 miles] a night. I started hallucinating and seeing visions of my daughter. It was that vivid I was putting my hand out to get a hold of her and she was talking to me."

Near the end of his ordeal, Ryan had lost 38 pounds and stumbled into the village of Abu Kamal, Syria. In 1995, he wrote an account of his ordeal entitled *The One That Got Away*, and he told his story to the *Daily Star Online* in 2018. "Every day, I would lie there and plan my route to get closer and closer to that Syrian border," he recalled. "All I thought for the seven days was 'Get across that border and I'll be safe' – but actually I wasn't. I ended up in the town right next to the border and a lynch mob tried to drag me back into Iraq."

Ryan managed to reach the local police station, but his fate remained unclear for a time as several men hustled him into a vehicle. "Driving in the car, we passed this large sign which said 'Baghdad' and the guys said, 'We're Iraqis.' They blindfolded me and I thought I'd been tricked, heading towards an Iraqi prison. As I sat there, I started running through in my head what would happen next, I'd get beaten up and interrogated, so it wasn't a surprise. As it was, they were having a joke and took me into Damascus."

Ryan added that the Syrians were gracious hosts and even bought him a suit before turning him over to the British embassy. He received the Military Medal for his exploits, despite the fact that suspicions regarding his story linger.

McNab, MacGown, Pring and Coburn were moved on several occasions during their six weeks of captivity and spent part of that time in the infamous Abu Ghraib prison.

The Bravo Two Zero team leader told a tale of excruciating physical torture and mental anguish. A few times McNab and Pring were able to make eye contact and encourage one another to keep going through winks and faint smiles. Still, McNab wrote, their captors were utterly brutal.

"As the kicks connected with my skull, there was a hissing, popping sound in my ears, and as I clenched my jaw I heard the bones creak together," he recalled. "I felt blood trickle out of my ears and down my face. I was worried I'd be left permanently deaf... They set at me with rifle butts and one particularly heavy blow caught me on the jaw. I felt my molars crack and splinter, and when the pain hit me I was down and screaming my head off.

"And so my ordeal went on and on, day after day, night after night. At one point we were driven out onto the streets and exhibited to roaring crowds of people – women with sticks, men with guns or stones, all waving pictures of Saddam Hussein."

McNab, MacGown and Pring were eventually released in early March, a few days after the Gulf War had ended. McNab received the Distinguished Conduct Medal, and Lane and Consiglio the Military Medal.

While there is no doubt that the brave SAS men of Bravo Two Zero engaged in their deployment with the intent to complete their mission, a series of unforeseen circumstances converged to create the ensuing catastrophe. Although their heroism cannot be denied, the accounts of those who participated and those who investigated reveal statements, eyewitness testimonies and theories that raise questions that may never be fully answered.

> "AS THE KICKS CONNECTED WITH MY SKULL, THERE WAS A HISSING, POPPING SOUND IN MY EARS. I FELT BLOOD TRICKLE OUT OF MY EARS AND DOWN MY FACE. I FELT MY MOLARS CRACK AND SPLINTER, AND WHEN THE PAIN HIT ME I WAS SCREAMING MY HEAD OFF"

"I THOUGHT 'GET ACROSS THAT BORDER AND I'LL BE SAFE' – BUT ACTUALLY I WASN'T. I ENDED UP IN THE TOWN RIGHT NEXT TO THE BORDER AND A LYNCH MOB TRIED TO DRAG ME BACK TO IRAQ"

*Above: The Bravo Two Zero Patrol Memorial bench is located at the Allied Special Forces Memorial Grove, National Memorial Arboretum, Alrewas, UK*

*Above: This memorial to Sergeant Vince Phillips of Bravo Two Zero is also located at the National Memorial Arboretum*

*Above: A close-up of Bravo Two Zero's plaque at the National Memorial Arboretum. It is dedicated to those who lost their lives in the mission*

# OPERATION DESERT STORM

In early 1991, an American-led United Nations coalition ended Iraq's occupation of Kuwait during the Gulf War with one of the most successful military campaigns of the 20th century

**WORDS: TOM GARNER**

Sometimes known as the "100-hour ground war", Operation Desert Storm was a short-lived, but highly effective campaign that defeated Saddam Hussein's Iraqi army, air force and navy in just 43 days. Fought in Kuwait, Iraq, Saudi Arabia and the Persian Gulf, Operation Desert Storm aimed to liberate Kuwait from occupying Iraqi forces. Conducted by a large international coalition led by the United States, the operation swiftly achieved its aims against Iraq's armed forces with a skilful use of combined numerical and technological superiority.

## Invasion of Kuwait

During 2-4 August 1990, Iraqi forces invaded their southern neighbouring country of Kuwait. At the beginning of the 1990s, Iraq had been ruled for over a decade by its president Saddam Hussein. An aggressive dictator who led the Arab nationalist Ba'ath Party, Saddam had already been embroiled in a long, regional war against Iran and committed genocide against Kurds who lived in Iraq.

The war with Iran in particular had placed huge financial strain on the Iraqi economy, with the country being US $14 million in debt to Kuwait. While the Kuwaitis demanded repayment, Saddam instead decided to occupy his neighbouring country to gain more control over its rich oil supply. During the two-day invasion, the Iraqis militarily overwhelmed the Kuwaiti armed forces in an action that immediately caused regional instability with global implications.

With Kuwait under occupation, Iraq directly threatened the security of its other, much larger neighbour, Saudi Arabia. If Saudi Arabia was also annexed, Saddam would then be in control of 40 percent of the world's oil reserves. The occupation of Kuwait provoked an international outcry with the United Nations immediately condemning the invasion and imposing economic sanctions on Iraq. The United States and United Kingdom also deployed soldiers and equipment to Saudi Arabia while encouraging other countries to contribute their own military support in the Persian Gulf.

*US President George HW Bush gives a speech from the Oval Office in the White House following the decision to launch Operation Desert Storm*

## Desert Shield

The UN demanded that Iraq immediately withdraw from Kuwait but Saddam refused. A standoff then ensued while the Americans led a 'defensive mission' to prevent an Iraqi invasion of Saudi Arabia. Authorised by US President George HW Bush, this mission was codenamed 'Operation Desert Shield'.

American troops and air forces were deployed to the country at the invitation of King Fahd of Saudi Arabia in August 1990 while two US Navy battle groups sailed to the Persian Gulf. Over half a million American military personnel were stationed in Saudi Arabia and the Persian Gulf while diplomatic tensions with Iraq continued to rise.

*Above: American soldiers take the Oath of Allegiance to the US Army on top of a destroyed Iraqi tank, 27 February 1991*

## Forming the Coalition

In late November 1990, the UN Security Council issued Resolution 678 that ordered Iraq to withdraw from Kuwait by 15 January 1991. In the event of Saddam not complying with the Resolution, the UN decided to form a huge coalition of allied nations that aimed to liberate Kuwait by force. This coalition was dominated by the United States but included 36 countries. It consisted of almost one million military personnel and huge numbers of aircraft, tanks and ships.

The vast majority of the soldiers were American with the United States providing almost 700,000 personnel. By contrast, the second and third largest contributing countries, Saudi Arabia and the United Kingdom, supplied 94,000 and 53,000 troops. Other countries included contingents from Egypt, France, Pakistan, Canada and Kuwait itself.

The Coalition consisted of a disparate array of partners. For example, Britain and Argentina had bitterly fought each other during the Falklands War in 1982 but they officially teamed up for the campaign. In contrast to the Americans, Denmark and New Zealand provided only 100 troops each while Hungary made the smallest contribution by deploying a team of just 40 medics.

In 20th century terms, the Coalition was the largest military alliance of its kind since the Second World War. In a historic irony, it even included a German Luftwaffe squadron that offered logistical air support. This was the first time that the recently reunified Germany had undertaken a military role since 1945 but its small aerial contribution was highly symbolic in terms of the country's military reintroduction to world affairs.

Although the UN coalition was huge, it faced Iraqi armed forces that had invaded Kuwait

with 100,000 men. By January 1991, Saddam also ordered the mobilisation of all of Iraq's military reserves, which boosted its armed forces to over 600,000 soldiers. With this total, Iraq controlled what was then the world's fourth-largest army. Nevertheless, the UN Coalition remained numerically and technically superior in an alliance that was built upon global cooperation against a country that was internationally isolated.

## Desert Storm

By 15 January 1991, Saddam showed no sign of removing Iraqi forces from Kuwait and when the UN Resolution 678 deadline passed, the Coalition moved to implement what was codenamed 'Operation Desert Storm'. Officially commencing on 17 January 1991, Desert Storm was simultaneously the UN move to liberate Kuwait and an aerial bombing campaign against Iraq.

The day before Desert Storm began in earnest, President Bush addressed the American people, "Our objectives are clear: Saddam Hussein's forces will leave Kuwait. The legitimate government of Kuwait will be restored to its rightful place, and Kuwait will once again be free."

The campaign against Iraqi forces was initially an intense, five-week bombardment of Iraqi military targets from air and sea. Coalition forces flew 100,000 aerial sorties and dropped almost 90,000 tons of bombs against Iraqi positions in both Kuwait and Iraq. Specifically, the Coalition's aim was to destroy the Iraqi Air Force, its anti-aircraft defences, command and communications facilities and other military targets such as Scud ballistic missile launchers. The Coalition was quickly able to gain air superiority over the numerically inferior Iraqi Air Force and by 23 February 1991, the

# AIRLAND BATTLE

After their defeat in the Vietnam War, the US Army began to study ways to better realign their organisational capabilities in response to real-world conflicts. They also studied other contemporary conflicts, such as the Yom Kippur War, where speed and technologically advanced firepower could decide conflicts in just a few battles. A military doctrine was subsequently developed between 1982-89 called 'AirLand Battle' that remains the US Army's basic doctrine for fighting wars.

AirLand Battle has four basic premises: 'Initiative', 'Agility', 'Depth' and 'Synchronisation'. 'Initiative' gives commanders the tactical edge in battle, with an emphasis on winning a war's first battle, even while being numerically outnumbered. 'Agility' is crucial for different forces to act faster than their enemy while 'Depth' requires a battle's "deeper" forces (such as logistics) to support the "closer" elements of close-combat forces. Meanwhile, 'Synchronisation' is defined as synchronising forces to provide the highest amount of combat power at decisive moments.

The doctrine was specifically developed for what was termed "mid or high-intensity conflict", such as regional wars or defending NATO. It was effectively proved during the Gulf War, which was a regional conflict conducted by UN Coalition forces that were dominated by NATO allies. Desert Storm incorporated some of the key tenets of AirLand Battle. This included Coalition armoured forces winning large tank battles despite being outnumbered, closely coordinating air and naval attacks and conducting all operations with great speed and superior firepower.

ground offensive element of Desert Storm was ready to commence.

During the aerial bombing campaign, the largest Coalition bombardment was an airstrike known as 'Package Q'. This saw 78 US Air Force aircraft attack several targets over the Iraqi capital of Baghdad, including a nuclear research centre. Meanwhile, Coalition naval forces destroyed the Iraqi Navy at sea in several engagements that saw the loss of over 100 Iraqi vessels, including 19 sunken ships.

## Ground Offensive

Despite the ferocity of the Coalition bombardments, Saddam remained defiant and the day after Operation Desert Storm began, he ordered the firing of missiles against Israel and Saudi Arabia.

These attacks resulted in no fatalities but the firing of the missiles, particularly against Israel, was politically charged. Several Arab nations, including Saudi Arabia, Egypt, Oman, Qatar and the United Arab Emirates were important members of the Coalition. However, they were also historically hostile to Israel. The Israelis were mindful of the importance of preserving the Coalition and so, despite their formidable military capabilities, they refrained from retaliating against Iraq.

Eleven days after attacking Israel, Saddam then ordered an invasion of Saudi Arabia. On 29 January 1991, three Iraqi divisions occupied the coastal Saudi city of Khafji just south of the Kuwaiti border. It became the site of the first ground engagement of the Gulf War with a three-day battle occurring between Iraqi and Saudi-led Coalition forces. The Coalition recaptured Khafji by 1 February 1991, although Saddam attempted to turn the event into a propaganda victory. Around the same time as the battle for Khafji, the Coalition increased their attacks against Iraqi ground forces to prepare for a ground assault. This included Special Forces who began to conduct

F-16A Fighting Falcon, F-15E Strike Eagle, and F-15C Eagle fighter jets fly over Kuwait's burning oil fields

USS Missouri fires her 16-inch guns at Iraqi targets along the northern Kuwaiti coast in the Persian Gulf, 6 February

Images: Getty Images, Alamy, Wiki

# DESERT STORM

*January-March 1991*

### Defining moment
## AIR CAMPAIGN
### 17 JANUARY - 23 FEBRUARY 1991

Operating over Iraq and Kuwait, the Coalition conducted an intense aerial bombardment against Iraqi military targets. Primarily focusing on destroying the Iraqi Air Force, the Coalition aerial forces were mostly American but also featured contributions from the United Kingdom, Saudi Arabia, Canada, France and Italy. Their combined forces of almost 2,800 aircraft were able to achieve air superiority in one week. The Coalition lost 75 aircraft but destroyed 254 Iraqi aircraft on the ground with an additional 36 being shot down during air-to-air combat. Approximately 10,000-12,000 Iraqis were killed as a result of the air campaign compared to just 46 Coalition air personnel.

### LIBERATION OF KUWAIT
The primary aim of Desert Storm's ground offensive was the liberation of Kuwait. With fighting occurring in both Kuwait and Iraq, the liberation only took four days to achieve after seven months of Iraqi occupation.
*24-28 FEBRUARY 1991*

### IRAQI MISSILE ATTACKS
Iraq launched 46 Scud ballistic missiles into Saudi Arabia against Coalition military targets and the capital Riyadh. Dozens of American soldiers were killed and many more wounded when a barracks was destroyed at Dhahran.
*18 JANUARY - 26 FEBRUARY 1991*

### PACKAGE Q AIRSTRIKE
'Package Q' was the largest airstrike of the war with the US Air Force attacking a number of targets in Baghdad, including their main objective of the Tuwaltha Nuclear Research Centre. 78 American aircraft participated but they failed to destroy Tuwaltha.
*19 January 1991*

### BATTLE OF BUBIYAN
The last and largest naval engagement of the war occurred off a Kuwaiti coastal island in the Persian Gulf. American, British and Canadian naval forces engaged and destroyed the remnants of the Iraqi Navy by sinking 21 vessels while suffering no losses.
*29 January - 2 February 1991*

### AMIRIYAH SHELTER BOMBING
The US Air Force conducted a controversial bombing attack over Baghdad when an air raid shelter was hit by two laser-guided bombs. At least 408 Iraqi civilians were killed with many foreign governments condemning the attack.
*13 FEBRUARY 1991*

*American soldiers assist and lead captured Iraqi soldiers away from the battlefield during Operation Desert Storm*

clandestine operations in Kuwait and Iraq. On 15 February 1991, the American Task Force 1-41 Infantry crossed the Saudi border into Iraq after a massive artillery bombardment. The Task Force began engaging with Iraqi ground forces two days later and quickly destroyed Iraq's artillery capabilities.

These American actions enabled Coalition forces to penetrate deeper into Iraq from 24 February but they were not immune to Iraqi counterattacks. On 25 February, a Scud missile hit a US Army barracks in Dhahran, Saudi Arabia that resulted in hundreds of casualties. 28 soldiers were killed with 260 more being wounded, including 110 hospitalisations.

This single missile attack accounted for more than a third of all American soldiers killed during the war. The following day after the Scud attack, Saddam announced that Iraqi forces would withdraw from Kuwait but he did not renounce Iraq's claim over the country. Coalition aircraft, led by American, British and French aerial forces (along with accompanying tank fire) bombed a convoy of retreating Iraqi troops and vehicles on the same day. Occurring on a motorway called Highway 80 in southern Iraq, the Coalition destroyed thousands of Iraqi vehicles while inflicting thousands of casualties on Iraqi soldiers who were either killed, wounded or captured. The ruined road would later become known as the "Highway of Death".

## Desert Sabre

At the same time as the destruction on Highway 80, the Coalition engaged in several battles against Iraqi forces in a subsidiary campaign of Desert Storm called 'Operation Desert Sabre'. During 26-27 February, several Iraqi armoured divisions were defeated by American and British forces at the Battle of 73 Easting. Named

## Defining moment
### "HIGHWAY OF DEATH" 25-27 FEBRUARY 1991

After the withdrawal from Kuwait, Coalition aerial forces bombed thousands of retreating Iraqi soldiers and vehicles along a six-lane motorway called Highway 80. Running from Kuwait into southern Iraq towards Basra, Highway 80 became a scene of carnage with the Coalition continuously carrying out bombing missions. A US Navy pilot described the Iraqis as "basically just sitting ducks", with the attack reaching a crescendo over a ten-hour period. By the end of the attack, hundreds of Iraqi soldiers were dead with over 2,000 of their vehicles being destroyed. 2,000 Iraqis were also captured while others escaped into the surrounding desert.

## Defining moment
### BATTLE OF NORFOLK 27 FEBRUARY 1991

Norfolk was the largest tank battle of the war with dozens of American, British and Iraqi armoured divisions participating. A continuation of the Battle of 73 Easting, Norfolk saw the destruction of even more Iraqi tanks and armoured vehicles and along with thousands of captured troops. The British 1st Armoured Division performed particularly well. Primarily using Challenger 1 tanks, the British travelled 217 miles in 97 hours and captured or destroyed around 300 Iraqi tanks. A single Challenger 1 even destroyed an Iraqi tank at a range of three miles (5,000 metres). This was the longest-distance tank-to-tank 'kill' in military history.

**BATTLE OF 73 EASTING**
One of several tank engagements that occurred in Iraq during 26-27 February 1991, 73 Easting saw American and British armoured forces destroy hundreds of Iraqi tanks and other vehicles at minimal cost to themselves.
*26-27 FEBRUARY 1991*

**BATTLE OF KUWAIT INTERNATIONAL AIRPORT**
The largest tank battle in the history of the US Marines saw American forces seize control of Kuwait International Airport from Iraqi forces. The victory at the airport then enabled the Americans to advance into Kuwait City.
*27 FEBRUARY 1991*

**CEASEFIRE**
US President George HW Bush declared a ceasefire after the liberation of Kuwait and the defeat of the Iraqi Army. President Bush made his declaration during a live TV broadcast from the Oval Office in the White House.
*27 FEBRUARY 1991*

**BATTLE OF RUMAILA**
Two days after the ceasefire, US Army forces controversially attacked a withdrawing column of Iraqi armoured forces in southern Iraq. The Iraqis suffered losses of over 700 killed, 3,000 captured and the destruction of hundreds of tanks and other armoured vehicles.
*2 MARCH 1991*

after a grid coordinate area in southeast Iraq, the battle saw hundreds of armoured vehicles engaging in the desert, although it was a very one-sided affair. For the loss of one tank, six killed and 19 wounded, the Coalition inflicted heavy losses on the Iraqis who suffered over 2,000 casualties and the loss of 420 vehicles, including 160 tanks.

Meanwhile, a tank battle also broke out on 27 February between American and Iraqi forces at Kuwait International Airport. Located almost ten miles south of Kuwait City, the battle was an engagement that was the largest tank battle in the history of the US Marines. It involved combined elements of 18 American and Iraqi divisions who fought to control access to the airport. While fighting was occurring at the airport, the US 1st and 2nd Marine Divisions met fierce Iraqi resistance as they entered Kuwait City. The Americans won the battle but the fighting resulted in severe damage to the airport and to important infrastructure in the Kuwaiti capital.

Shortly after 73 Easting and Kuwait International Airport, American and British forces again fought another tank engagement during 27-28 February in the southern Iraqi Al Muthanna Province in what became known as the Battle of Norfolk. Similar to 73 Easting, 'Norfolk' was a codename for an objective that included a road intersection, nearby desert trails and an Iraqi supply depot that was defended by armoured vehicles.

The order of battle for Norfolk was formidable. The US Army VII Corps consisted of four divisions (including two armoured divisions) and an artillery brigade as well as the British 1st Armoured Division. Opposing them were large Iraqi forces that included eight divisions of armoured vehicles and infantry, along with four more armoured and mechanised brigades. The opposing sides created a combined total of thousands of tanks and soldiers with Norfolk proving to be the largest tank battle of the Gulf War.

Like 73 Easting, Norfolk was another one-sided engagement. The Americans and British incurred light casualties of 51 soldiers killed and over 137 wounded with the loss of only four tanks and seven IFVs (Infantry Fighting Vehicles). By contrast, the Iraqis again suffered severe losses. Approximately 850 Iraqi tanks and hundreds of other vehicles were destroyed while over 7,000 soldiers were captured. Norfolk became the second largest tank battle in American history after the Battle of the Bulge during the Second World War. It also turned out to be the final battle of the war.

## "Kuwait is liberated"

The results of these various battles that were fought simultaneously, or in quick succession, were the climactic engagements of Desert Storm. The operation had resulted in the collapse of Iraqi military forces and, with the liberation of Kuwait City, President Bush announced a ceasefire of hostilities on 27 February 1991.

Speaking to the American people on television, Bush declared, "Kuwait is liberated. Iraq's army is defeated. Our military objectives are met. Kuwait is once more in the hands of Kuwaitis, in control of their own destiny.

Images: Getty images, Alamy

We share in their joy, a joy tempered only by our compassion for their ordeal. Tonight, the Kuwaiti flag once again flies above the capital of a free and sovereign nation."

In the same address, Bush also acknowledged that Desert Storm's success was a collective effort, "Seven months ago, America and the world drew a line in the sand. We declared that the aggression against Kuwait would not stand. And tonight, America and the world have kept their word…No one country can claim this victory as its own. It was not only a victory for Kuwait but a victory for all the Coalition partners. This is a victory for the United Nations, for all mankind, for the rule of law, and for what is right."

Bush's address came six weeks after the beginning of Desert Storm and on 28 February, Iraq announced that it would accept all UN resolutions regarding the conflict. A few days later, the Iraqis accepted the terms of a ceasefire agreement presented on 3 March by the Coalition commander, US General Norman Schwarzkopf. One month later, the UN adopted Resolution 687 with terms that Iraq was expected to comply with after losing the war. A demilitarised zone and reinforced barrier was established along the Iraq-Kuwait border with Saddam Hussein being forced to recognise Kuwait's independence. He was also required to return Kuwaiti property and end his programme for weapons of mass destruction. Nevertheless, despite his comprehensive defeat, Saddam remained in power until the American-led invasion of Iraq in 2003.

## Casualties

The detailed planning that went into Operation Desert Shield meant that Operation Desert Storm resulted in relatively few casualties for the Coalition. 292 Coalition personnel (excluding Kuwaitis) were killed with a further 776 wounded. Kuwait suffered losses of 420 soldiers killed and 12,000 captured while over 1,000 of the country's civilians also died. The human and material costs for Iraq were much greater. Estimates for its casualty figures vary but they range between at least 30,000 and as high as 100,000. Around 80,000-175,000 soldiers were captured with its armed forces also incurring the loss of over 3,000 tanks, 2,000 artillery pieces, 110 aircraft and dozens of ships. Iraqi civilians also suffered with over 3,600 killed.

For the Coalition and particularly the USA, Desert Storm was an extremely successful campaign from a military perspective. On the 30th anniversary of the operation in 2021, it was described by the US General Accountability Office as "perhaps the most successful war fought in the 20th century".

## "KUWAIT IS LIBERATED. IRAQ'S ARMY IS DEFEATED. OUR MILITARY OBJECTIVES ARE MET. KUWAIT IS ONCE MORE IN THE HANDS OF KUWAITIS"

British engineers from the 7th Armoured Brigade detonate an Iraqi mine shield in the Saudi Arabian desert, 7 January 1991

# F-16
# FIGHTING FALCON

Arguably the world's most successful jet fighter, the Fighting Falcon has served in nations around the world, in conflicts spanning decades

**WORDS:** STUART HADAWAY

*The F-16 was adopted by the USAF display team the Thunderbirds in 1983*

### GAPING AIR INTAKE
A distinctive feature is the unsightly and seemingly ungainly air intake under the cockpit. It is set far enough back to reduce drag and minimise air-flow loss. A splitter plate is used to control air flow.

## "THE F-16 WOULD LATER BE DEVELOPED INTO A HIGHLY CAPABLE ALL-WEATHER MULTI-ROLE AIRCRAFT"

The General Dynamics (later Lockheed, then Lockheed Martin) F-16 Fighting Falcon is widely regarded as the world's most successful jet fighter. Originally designed in the early 1970s to meet a US requirement for a low-cost, low-weight fighter, it came after decades of building heavy fighters designed primarily as interceptors or strike attack aircraft. Experience in the Vietnam War convinced the military of the need for a pure-bred dogfighter – lean, light and agile. Ironically, from its inception as a day fighter, the F-16 would later be developed into a highly capable all-weather multi-role aircraft with a formidable ground-attack ability.

Even as the US Air Force (USAF) was announcing the adoption of the F-16 in 1975, a European group including Belgium, the Netherlands, Denmark and Norway also declared their intention to purchase it. It would be the start of a prodigious overseas career for the aircraft. During its history, around 25 other countries would operate the F-16 (and several more have considered ordering the type), and the aircraft would be licence-built in several of those countries. Both Israel and Pakistan would use the type in combat before the US did, and, with over 4,500 built, it continues to be one of the most numerous and widely used fighters in the world.

# GENERAL DYNAMICS
## F-16 FIGHTING FALCON

| COMMISSIONED | 1972 |
|---|---|
| ORIGIN | USA |
| LENGTH | 49FT 5IN (15.06M) |
| WINGSPAN | 32FT 8IN (9.96M) |
| ENGINE | 1 X GENERAL ELECTRIC F110-GE-129 OR PRATT & WHITNEY F100-PW-229 AFTERBURNING TURBOFAN |
| CREW | 1 |
| PRIMARY WEAPON | UP TO 16,975LB (7,700KG) OF AIR-TO-AIR MISSILES, BOMBS OR ROCKETS |
| SECONDARY WEAPON | M61A1 VULCAN ROTARY CANNON |

**VARIABLE-CAMBER WINGS**
Flaperons along the leading and trailing edges of the wings are automatically controlled by the on-board computer, varying the camber of the wings to maximise performance.

**CLOSE-SET UNDERCARRIAGE**
The F-16 has a close-set and surprisingly simple tricycle undercarriage. In order to keep the wing thin, it folds into the lower fuselage.

**FULLY MOVING STABILISERS**
After some early stability issues, the F-16 was fitted with larger and fully moving horizontal stabilisers, improving performance at high angles of attack, assisting with stall recovery and aiding faster take-offs.

*Left: A Turkish Air Force F-16 demonstrates its self-defence suite*

Illustration: Nicholas Forder

# ARMAMENT

The F-16 has a 20mm M61A1 Vulcan six-barrelled cannon in the fuselage to the left of the cockpit, and also carries a fearsome array of other weaponry. Initially designed to carry two AIM-9 Sidewinder missiles, one on each wing tip, continuous developments have seen the number of hard-points rise to 11, of which nine can carry ordnance (the others carrying sensors and other systems) or external fuel tanks. Up to 16,975lb (7,700kg) of air-to-air or air-to-ground missiles, iron and smart bombs, or rockets can be carried to meet almost any mission requirement.

*Below: US Air Force Major Todd Pierce, a pilot with the 451st Expeditionary Fighter Squadron, inspects the bombs and missiles on an F-16C Fighting Falcon, at Kandahar Airfield, Afghanistan, April 2012*

*Right: An F-16 drops two laser-guided bombs over a range*

"UP TO 16,975LB (7,700KG) OF AIR-TO-AIR OR AIR-TO-GROUND MISSILES, IRON AND SMART BOMBS, OR ROCKETS CAN BE CARRIED TO MEET ALMOST ANY MISSION REQUIREMENT"

*The F-16 has nine weapons pylons – one on each wing tip, three under each wing and one under the fuselage. The wing tip pylons are typically used for air-to-air missiles*

# DESIGN

With wing-body blending and a cropped delta wing swept back at 40°, the F-16 has a sleek look marred only by the gaping air intake under the nose. Light and strong, it can perform at up to 9G and exceed Mach 2, with its agility improved by 'relaxed static stability'. This essentially means that the aircraft is inherently unstable, with numerous adjustable sections around the wings and fuselage automatically trimming the aircraft in normal flight. Every aspect of the aircraft is designed with ease of access and maintenance in mind.

*Right: The F-16 utilises a number of automatic, computer-controlled systems to maximise performance by physically changing the shape of the wings and control surfaces*

# ENGINE

The Falcon was originally fitted with the Pratt & Whitney F100-PW-200 afterburning turbofan, a development of the -100 that was built for the F-15 Eagle. Rated at 23,830lbf (106kN), the engine initially had reliability issues but subsequent developments of the -220 and -220E greatly improved it. Today, F-16s tend to have the General Electric F110-GE-12, rated at 29,388lbf (131.61kN) with afterburner, or the Pratt & Whitney F110-PW-229, rated at 29,160lbf (129.7kN) with afterburner.

*Below: Engine change on an F-16; both engine and airframe are designed for ease of replacement*

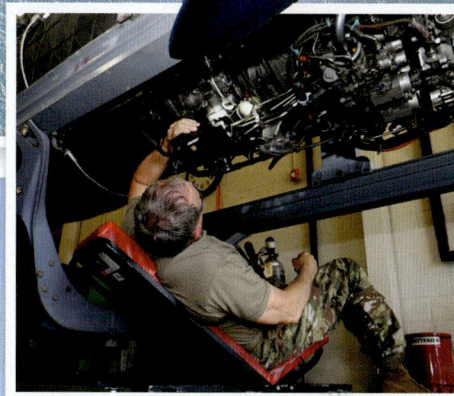

*Above: Most parts of engine and avionics are easily accessible through exterior panels*

Images Alamy

*The F-16's distinctive bubble canopy provides the pilot with excellent visibility*

# COCKPIT

One of the F-16's most distinctive features is the high bubble canopy. Frameless and reinforced to protect against bird strikes, the bulging sides combined with very high-set seat provide a 360° view, with a remarkable 40° down-view. The pilot's ejector seat is also set at a 30° angle, helping them cope with high-G manoeuvres. Primary flight controls are similarly adapted, with a side-mounted control column on the right and throttles on the left, both fitted with numerous other controls which the pilot might otherwise struggle to reach while under high-G.

*Above: Interior of an F-16 cockpit, with the side-mounted control column allowing easier control under high-G*

*Two USAF F-16s on patrol over Iraq, 2020*

## SERVICE HISTORY

Entering service with the USAF in 1978, the F-16 quickly spread around the world. It was used by the USAF over Iraq from 1991 onwards, and with the USAF and various European forces over the Balkans, Afghanistan and Libya. The type has also seen combat over the Pakistan-India border, Israel's borders, over Syria with the Turkish Air Force, and over the Sinai with the Egyptians, as well over Yemen with the Moroccan and Bahraini air forces. Easy to maintain, highly capable and now fully adapted for strike operations, the F-16 has proven an extremely popular and cost-effective force-multiplier for many nations.

The F-16 remains in production even after 50 years, and several Eastern European countries have either ordered or stated an intent to order them to replace their slightly younger Mikoyan MiG-29s. Ukraine is one of those countries, with the support of Britain, the Netherlands, Denmark and Belgium to train their pilots.

*Above: An Israeli F-16 takes off for a patrol over the Negev Desert, 2008*

"EASY TO MAINTAIN, HIGHLY CAPABLE AND NOW FULLY ADAPTED FOR STRIKE OPERATIONS, THE F-16 HAS PROVEN AN EXTREMELY POPULAR AND COST-EFFECTIVE FORCE-MULTIPLIER FOR MANY NATIONS"

*Below: Royal Danish Air Force F-16 in low-level flight over California's Mojave Desert*

*Below: An F-16 Fighting Falcon receives fuel from a KC-135 Stratotanker*

Images Alamy

# THE BATTLE OF KHAFJI

Controversially Saddam Hussein embarrassed the Coalition
by seizing a Saudi town, from right under their very noses

The battle of Khafji was to be one of national prestige and as the area was Saudi soil, it was felt that the Saudi National Guard, with support from Qatari troops, should be given the role of driving the Iraqis out. These forces were under General Khalid, backed by US Marines and Coalition airpower. "Two British advisers from the British Military Mission to the National Guard accompanied the engagement," Ambassador Alan Munro later admitted.

If the Coalition had given Saddam a breathing space, there is every reason to believe that he could have turned Khafji into a fortified stronghold. The Coalition knew from the Iran-Iraq War that the Iraqis were moderately competent in the offensive; of greater concern was the fact that they had fought eight years of almost continuous defensive action against the Iranians. The Iraqi Army was skilled in constructing defensive positions, berms, minefields and laying down artillery fire.

## Jet strikes

At first the Saudis were slow in responding to Saddam's invasion, blaming the lack of adequate air support from the US Marines. Once the Cobra helicopter gunship and Harrier and A-10 jet strikes got going they accounted for about 35 Iraqi tanks, alleviating the threat to the relief force. These air attacks also served to slow down the Saudis who withdrew two-three kilometres every time there was an air engagement. On their initial advance the Saudis successfully secured the surrender of five Iraqi tanks and six APCs outside the town, their crews demoralised by the airstrikes. Other units were not so keen to give up and one Saudi armoured vehicle was credited with knocking out eight Iraqi tanks.

In light of the Iraqi artillery fire it was decided to launch the first assault under the cover of darkness, potentially a tricky operation despite

the use of modern technology such as the thermal imagers. On the night of 30/31 January the Saudi and Qatari forces (though they were largely Pakistanis serving in these units) moved up to their jump off points. Coalition aircraft had by this stage silenced most of the Iraqi armour foolish enough to be visible. They also bombed two divisions of Saddam's 3rd Corps detected inside Kuwait gathering for a follow-on attack at Khafji. One strike by three American B-52 bombers reportedly destroyed 80 vehicles.

## Anti-tank fire

Under cover of a supporting barrage the Saudis gained a lodgement in the southern end of the town. Inaccurate and sporadic small arms and anti-tank fire greeted their attack. The Iraqis recovering from the first clash proved to be

*A vehicle destroyed during the Battle of Khafji*

An LAV-AT anti-tank missile carrier was destroyed by friendly anti-tank missile during the Battle of Khafji

Source: Wiki / PD Gov

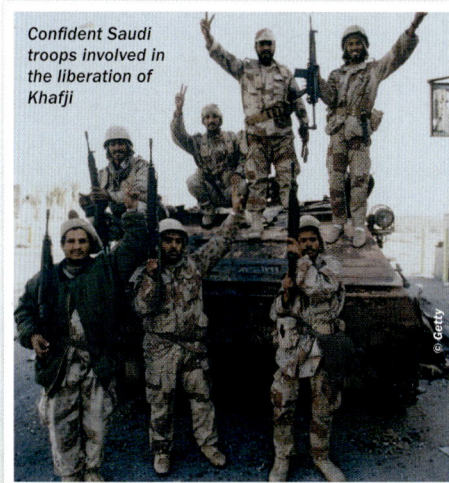

Confident Saudi troops involved in the liberation of Khafji

© Getty

resilient and some of their remaining soldiers had to be cleared from the town's outlying buildings one by one. Nevertheless, in the chaos others quickly threw down their arms, perhaps realising they were cut off and that resistance was now futile.

The third day of fighting for Khafji lasted 12 hours. When eventually the Iraqi snipers had been silenced it was discovered the Iraqis had lost in and around the town at least 40 dead (some reports state as many as 300 and it is thought the Saudis may have played down the death toll), 35 wounded, 463 prisoners and up to 80 armoured vehicles. Several of Saddam's Chinese supplied APCs were found knocked out in the streets, lost either to the Coalition's fighter-bombers or artillery. The entire Iraqi garrison had been destroyed.

## Morale boost

First blood had gone to the Coalition forces and the SANG had given a good if patchy account of itself. Furthermore, the Coalition was able to heave a sigh of relief that the urban battlefield had not turned into a costly bloodbath and a media disaster. This proved a major morale boost for the untested Saudi armed forces and showed they could conduct themselves well. In three days the Saudi forces lost 18 killed and 32 wounded, three tanks and an anti-tank launcher. During that period according to the Saudis the Iraqis lost 11 tanks while 51 APCs were destroyed and 19 APCs captured.

Although only a minor engagement in the overall scheme of things, Khafji echoed German attempts to move their armour to the Normandy bridgehead in 1944. If Saddam could have widened the battle by bringing up his follow-on forces and offered some token air cover the fight may not have gone so easily for the Coalition. It is possible the Americans would have had to divert more troops to help the Saudis, distracting them from the left hook. Without air support the Iraqis' offensive manoeuvring was totally compromised.

It was air power and artillery that were to dominate at Khafji and they were a dominant feature of the whole campaign. Nonetheless, Saddam's seizure of Khafji before the Coalition was ready to conduct its ground offensive proved an embarrassing if brief setback.

**"ONE SAUDI ARMOURED VEHICLE WAS CREDITED WITH KNOCKING OUT EIGHT IRAQI TANKS"**

# T-72
# MAIN BATTLE TANK

### This Soviet-design emerged during the Cold War and continues as a mainstay of many armies around the world

**WORDS:** MICHAEL E. HASKEW

The T-72 main battle tank is the most commonly employed armoured fighting vehicle in the world today – a relic of the Cold War that is still in frontline use in war zones such as Ukraine. Emerging from Soviet design instructions that would leverage existing technology available in the late 1960s and incorporate financially feasible improvements, the T-72 was a concurrent project along with the T-64 main battle tank. While the T-64 was intended for frontline Red Army troops to counter NATO forces in Europe, the T-72 was a cheaper alternative that was intended to equip further Red Army units and Warsaw Pact nations while providing a strong entrée into the global arms export market.

The T-72 was the result of a design competition that pitted Leonard Kartsev and the Uralvagon KB project based in Nizhny Tagil against the Morozov KB project under Alexander Morozov in Kharkov. The primary goal of the competition was to develop a cost-efficient replacement for the aging fleet of Communist Bloc T-54 and T-55 main battle tanks that had been in service since the late 1940s. The T-62 and T-64 were initial attempts but success was limited due to high costs, complex attributes and premature entry into production. The shortcomings of the T-62 and T-64 included limited production numbers and some antipathy from Warsaw Pact countries. The concurrent development of the T-72 was a compromise in cost, firepower and technology. Its longevity in service validates this approach, although the combat effectiveness of the T-72, nicknamed Ural, is a subject of debate.

### MAIN ARMAMENT
The T-72's 2A46M smoothbore cannon has been in service since 1970 and can fire a variety of armour-piercing and high-explosive rounds.

### HULL ARMOUR
The tank's front glacis is up to 7.9in (200mm) thick, while the sides are 2-3.2in (50-80mm). Explosive Reactive Armour (ERA) was added to later iterations of the tank.

*Right: The T-72 was a compromise in cost, firepower and technology, and its battlefield performance is fiercely debated*

## T-72 MAIN BATTLE TANK

| | |
|---|---|
| COMMISSIONED | 1973 |
| ORIGIN | SOVIET UNION |
| LENGTH | 30.3FT (9.24M) |
| RANGE | 290 MILES (467KM) |
| ENGINE | 780HP, 12-CYLINDER W-46 DIESEL |
| CREW | 3 |
| PRIMARY WEAPON | 125MM SMOOTHBORE 2A46M CANNON |
| SECONDARY WEAPON | .50-CAL (12.7MM) PINTLE MOUNT & 7.62MM COAXIAL MOUNT MACHINE GUNS |
| ARMOUR | UP TO 7.9IN (200MM) FRONT GLACIS; SIDE PLATES 2-3.2IN (50MM-80MM) |

### POWERPLANT

The 780hp, 12-cylinder W-46 diesel engine (later upgraded to 840hp) appeared underpowered yet was sufficient to give the relatively light tank excellent speed and manoeuvrability.

## "THE T-72 MAIN BATTLE TANK IS THE MOST COMMONLY EMPLOYED ARMOURED FIGHTING VEHICLE IN THE WORLD TODAY"

### TURRET

The elliptical, 'frying pan-shaped' turret has a low silhouette characteristic of previous Soviet tank design. Shells are stored in the turret, making the tank vulnerable if hit.

### SECONDARY ARMAMENT

A pintle-mount .50-cal (12.7mm) machine gun sits atop the T-72 main battle tank's turret. The vehicle is also armed with a coaxial-mount machine gun parallel to the main weapon.

*Explosive Reactive Armour (ERA) is easily visible on the turret and hull of this T-72 in service with the Indian Army*

Illustration: Nicholas Forder

*Above: A destroyed T-72 tank just outside Benghazi, Libya, 2011*

## ARMAMENT

Developed by the Spetstekhnika Design Bureau in Yekaterinburg in the 1960s originally for the T-64, the 2A46M 4.9in (125mm) smoothbore cannon has been in service since 1970 and served as the primary weapon of a series of Soviet and Russian main battle tanks. Capable of firing a variety of armour-piercing and high-explosive rounds, the smoothbore was superior to the 4.2in (105mm) rifled weapons of Western main battle tanks at the time of its introduction. Its short barrel life was addressed in a subsequent upgrade, while future NATO tanks adopted larger-calibre main weapons to counter the 2A46M. The cannon has also been manufactured in Ukraine and China.

## ENGINE

The 780hp, 12-cylinder W-46 diesel engine was much quieter than earlier diesels installed in the T-62, creating lower vibration throughout the vehicle and diminishing smoke output. It was capable of operating on benzene and kerosene when other fuel supplies were unavailable. The W-46 was based on the Second World War-era V-12 engine that powered the T-34 medium tank, which contributed to the interchanging of parts and availability of components for routine maintenance. Although the engine appeared underpowered for the size of the T-72 by Western standards, the overall light weight of the hull compensated, resulting in a highly manoeuvrable tank. Among other powerplant and drivetrain changes, the engine was upgraded to an 840hp variant in 1985.

*Tank crew starting the T-72 engine. Ukraine. Donetsk region. December 4 2022*

## DESIGN

The design of the T-72 was not a further development of the T-62 or T-64 – it was concurrent with them. The design retained the characteristic low silhouette of earlier Soviet tanks along with the elliptical, 'frying pan-shaped' turret; intentionally cramped crew capacity; and the characteristic long barrel of its main weapon, which gives the entire vehicle a somewhat forward-sloping appearance. Soviet tank designers stressed speed and manoeuvrability in line with the heritage of the classic T-34 design of the Great Patriotic War, prioritising battlefield survivability over inherent crew comfort, and the low-profile helped keep the vehicle's weight somewhat below that of contemporary NATO main battle tanks.

*The T-72 main battle tank is characterised by its low profile and its main weapon's long barrel*

## "SOVIET TANK DESIGNERS STRESSED SPEED AND MANOEUVRABILITY IN LINE WITH THE HERITAGE OF THE CLASSIC T-34"

*A T-72 is pictured during a training exercise in Ukraine, March 2023*

## SERVICE HISTORY

Since its introduction in 1973, the T-72 tank – in numerous variants – has been fielded by the armies of approximately 40 countries. Manufactured both for the Soviet army and in variants intended specifically for the export market, more than 25,000 have been produced. The T-72 has been built under licence in Poland, Czechoslovakia, the former Yugoslavia and India. Through the years, various upgrades have included Explosive Reactive Armour (ERA); Nuclear, Biological and Chemical warfare (NBC) equipment; and various infrared fire control systems.

The combat record of the T-72 is reflective of its sale on the world arms market. The Iraqi armed forces deployed the tank with some success against the Iranians in their 1980-88 war, while the tank was also deployed in the 1982 Lebanon conflict, the 1991 Gulf War and the 2003 US-led invasion of Iraq. During the Gulf War and the Iraq invasion, the export versions of the T-72 fared poorly against US M1A1 main battle tanks and the anti-tank weapons mounted on helicopters and fixed-wing aircraft.

Currently, various iterations of the T-72 are involved with both Russian and Ukrainian forces in the war in Ukraine. Western intelligence sources report that the Russian army is upgrading older T-72s to the B3 specification, but losses to artillery and hunter-killer infantry teams with anti-tank weapons are believed to be quite high.

"VARIOUS UPGRADES HAVE INCLUDED EXPLOSIVE REACTIVE ARMOUR (ERA); NUCLEAR, BIOLOGICAL AND CHEMICAL WARFARE (NBC) EQUIPMENT; AND VARIOUS INFRARED FIRE CONTROL SYSTEMS"

*Since its introduction in 1973, more than 25,000 T-72 tanks have been produced*

# CREW COMPARTMENT

Characteristically, the crew compartment of the T-72 main battle tank was not built for comfort. The chassis of the tank was divided into three sections, the crew compartment in the centre. The driver was situated forward with limited visibility through only a single periscope and, unlike Western tank designs that utilised a wheel or yoke, a system of tillers was used to steer. Along with the manual transmission, the driver was fully occupied while the tank was in motion. An automatic loader eliminated the need for a fourth crewman, and the commander was positioned in the turret to the right beneath a rotating cupola, while the gunner was seated in the turret to the left. The maximum height for T-72 crewmen is believed to be 5ft 9in (1.75m).

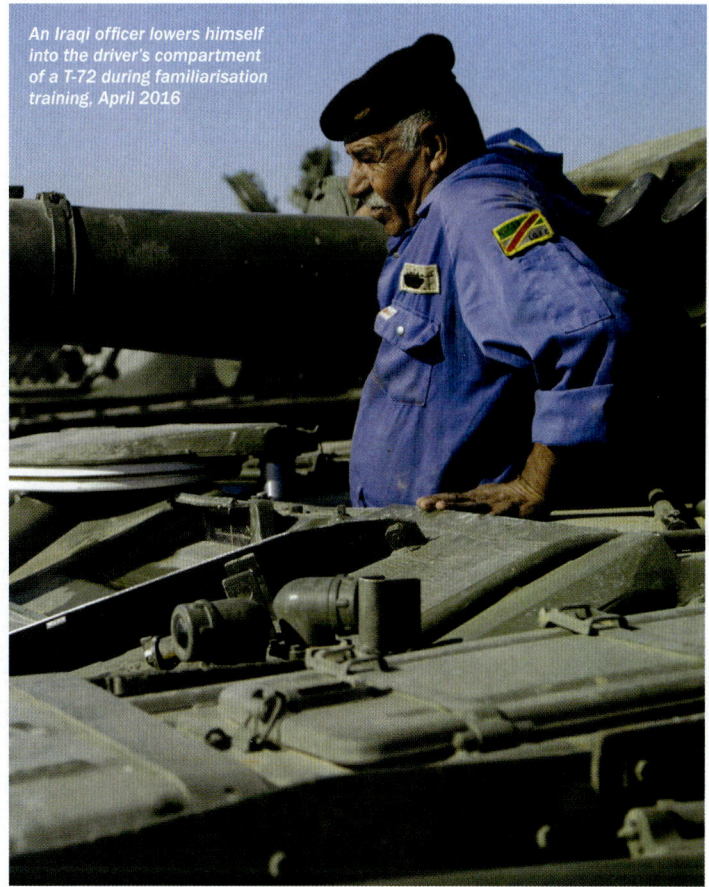

*Above: A pro-Russian separatist stands in front of a T-72 tank at a checkpoint in Enakieve, 25 kilometers from the eastern Ukrainian city of Debaltseve, on 29 January, 2015*

*Below: Upgraded variants such as this captured T-72B3 are reported by Western intelligence sources to be in service with the Russian army in Ukraine*

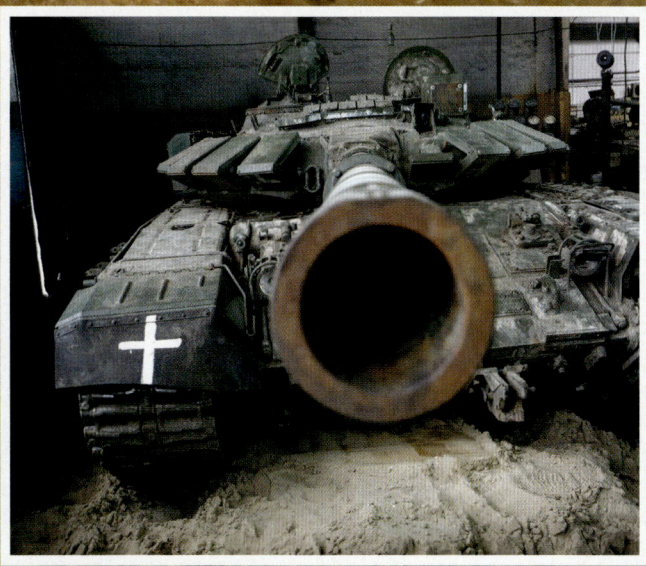

*An Iraqi officer lowers himself into the driver's compartment of a T-72 during familiarisation training, April 2016*

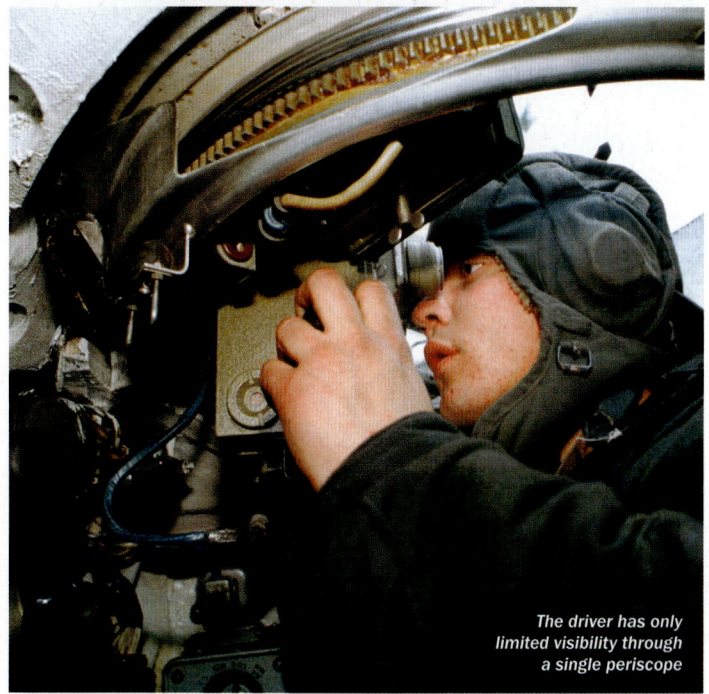

*The driver has only limited visibility through a single periscope*

Images Alamy, Getty, Wiki / PD / Gov

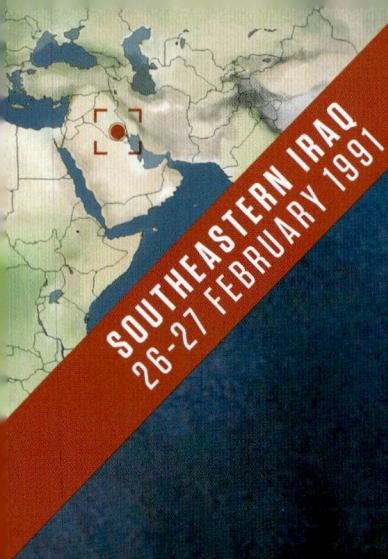

Great Battles

# 73 EASTING

During Operation Desert Storm, elements of the US 2nd Armored Cavalry Regiment annihilated Iraqi tanks and fighting vehicles in a decisive battle

WORDS MICHAEL E. HASKEW

## OPPOSING FORCES

🇺🇸 **VS** 🇮🇶

| EAGLE TROOP, 2ND SQUADRON, 2ND ARMORED CAVALRY REGIMENT | TAWAKALNA MECHANIZED DIVISION REPUBLICAN GUARD BRIGADE |
|---|---|
| **LEADER** Captain HR McMaster | **LEADER** Major Mohammed |
| **TANKS** 9 x M1A1 | **TANKS** 70 x T-72 |
| **CFV** 12 x M3 Bradley | **AFV** 80 x BMP |
| **TROOPS** 130 | **TROOPS** 2,300 |
| **FIRE SUPPORT** 2 x 120mm mortars | **ARTILLERY** 20 various systems |

Images: Alamy, Getty

On 2 August 1990, Saddam Hussein ordered his army to invade neighbouring Kuwait. The unprovoked attack and brutal Iraqi occupation sparked outrage, international condemnation and a demand from the United Nations that Iraq withdraw immediately. Three days after the invasion, US President George HW Bush declared: "This will not stand, this Iraqi aggression against Kuwait."

During the subsequent Operation Desert Shield, the United States led a coalition of 35 nations in a build-up of overwhelming military capability on land, sea and air in preparation for the forcible ejection of the Iraqi Army from Kuwait. Within five months, the coalition had assembled more than 950,000 troops, 3,000 tanks, 1,800 aircraft and 2,200 artillery pieces – along with considerable naval fire support capability – to oppose the Iraqi forces, which numbered over one million troops, 5,500 tanks and 700 aircraft. On 17 January 1991, the coalition unleashed a torrent of cruise missiles launched from submarines and warships, along with a sustained aerial bombing campaign designed to degrade the Iraqi combat effectiveness prior to the initiation of ground operations.

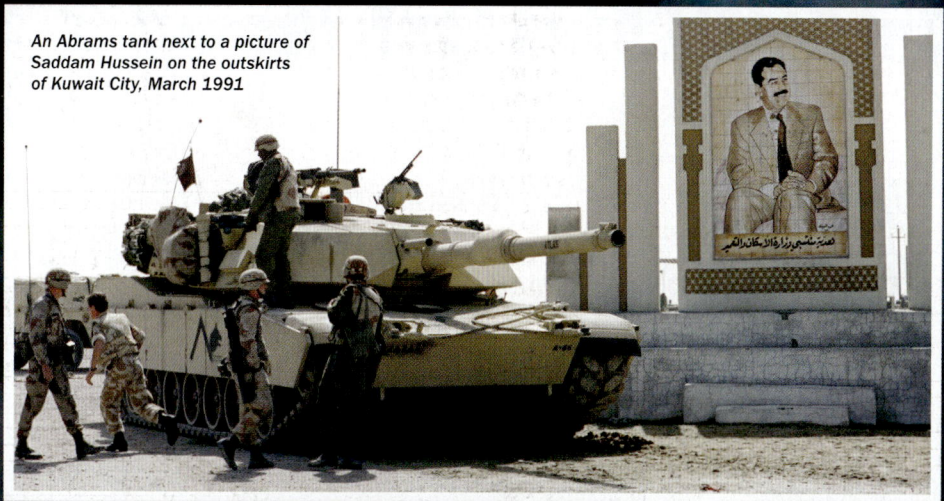

An Abrams tank next to a picture of Saddam Hussein on the outskirts of Kuwait City, March 1991

38 days later, on 24 February 1991, Coalition ground forces commenced operations against the Iraqi military in earnest, intent on driving the invading aggressors from Kuwait and destroying their fighting capability, particularly that of the elite Republican Guard divisions – well-trained and equipped troops, some of whom were veterans of the Iran-Iraq War of 1980-88.

US General Norman Schwarzkopf, commander of the Coalition forces, devised a plan to accomplish the mission at hand. Utilising overwhelming air power to erode Iraqi command and control and reduce enemy combat capability, he also employed a spectacularly successful campaign of deception. While large-scale amphibious manoeuvres complemented by covert

## "THIS WILL NOT STAND, THIS IRAQI AGGRESSION AGAINST KUWAIT"
### President George HW Bush

An Iraqi tank stands abandoned as burning oil wells fill the sky with smoke

# THE BATTLE OF 73 EASTING

## 26TH FEBRUARY 1991

## 01 POSITIONED FOR ACTION

Prior to the initiation of the 100-hour ground war during Operation Desert Storm, the coalition amasses overwhelming firepower and trains extensively, preparing for the execution of its 'Hail Mary' plan and a crushing victory over Iraqi forces.

## 02 RAPID ADVANCE

In the vanguard of VII Corps, the 2nd Armored Cavalry Regiment (2nd ACR) encounters sporadic resistance through the opening phase of the advance into Iraq, brushing aside opposition in its scouting role.

## 03 RECONNAISSANCE REWARDED

On the second day of Operation Desert Storm, Ghost Troop, 2nd ACR, destroys a dozen Iraqi armoured fighting vehicles and gathers intelligence indicating that coalition forces are within the operations zone of the Republican Guard.

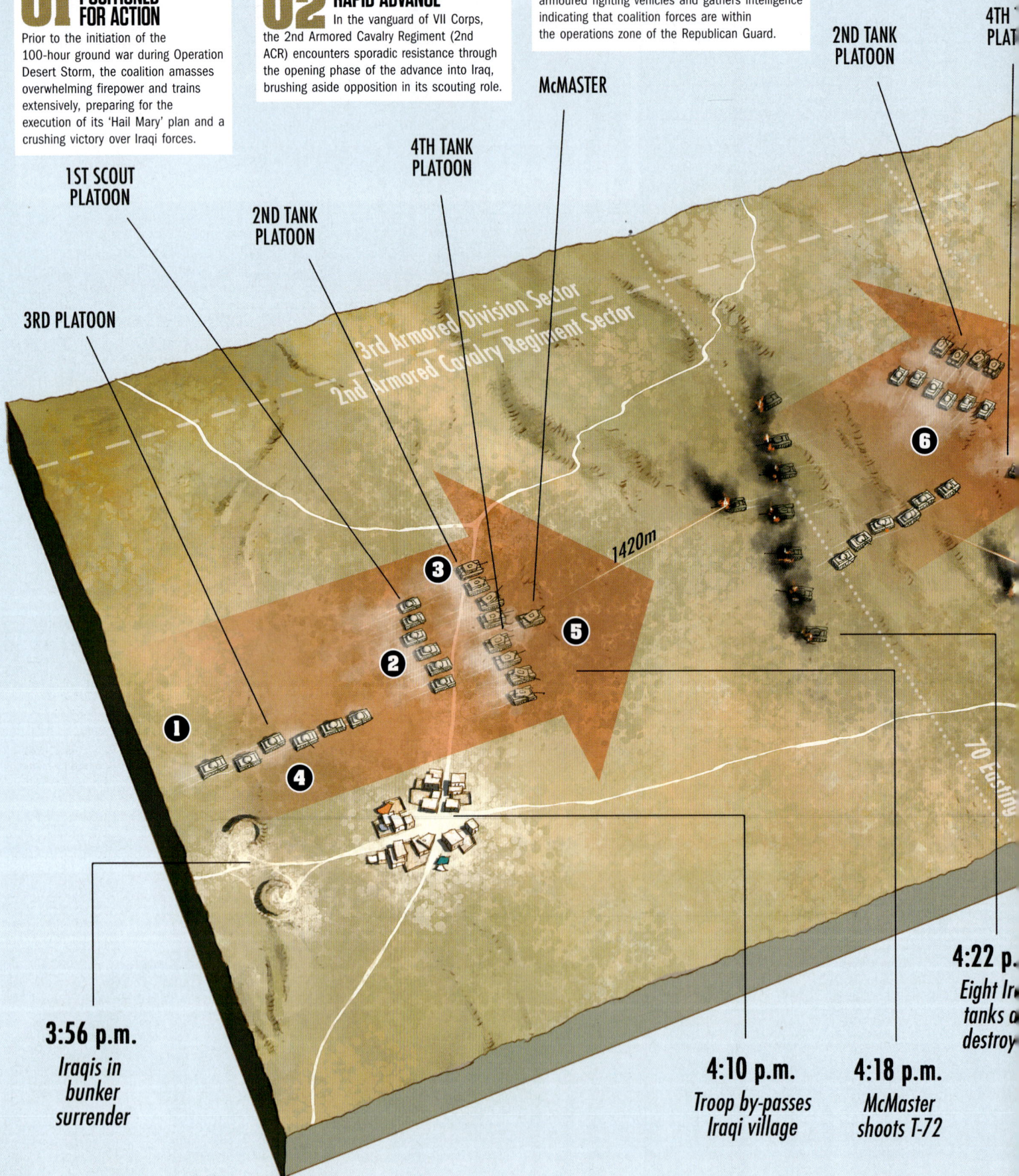

McMASTER

4TH TANK PLATOON

2ND TANK PLATOON

4TH PLAT...

1ST SCOUT PLATOON

2ND TANK PLATOON

3RD PLATOON

3rd Armored Division Sector

2nd Armored Cavalry Regiment Sector

1420m

70 Easting

**3:56 p.m.**

*Iraqis in bunker surrender*

**4:10 p.m.**

*Troop by-passes Iraqi village*

**4:18 p.m.**

*McMaster shoots T-72*

**4:22 p.m.**

*Eight Ir... tanks a... destroy...*

## Area of Detail

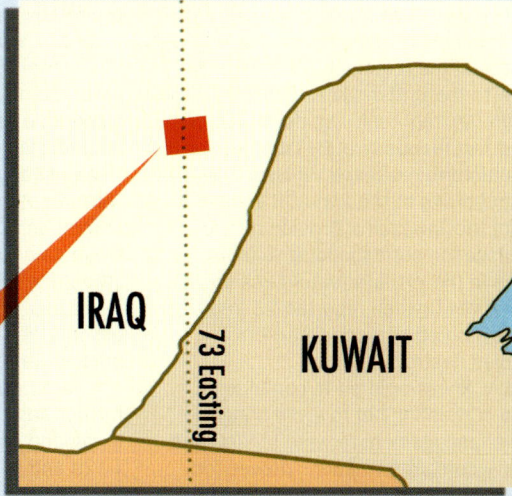

COIL OF 17
IRAQI TANKS

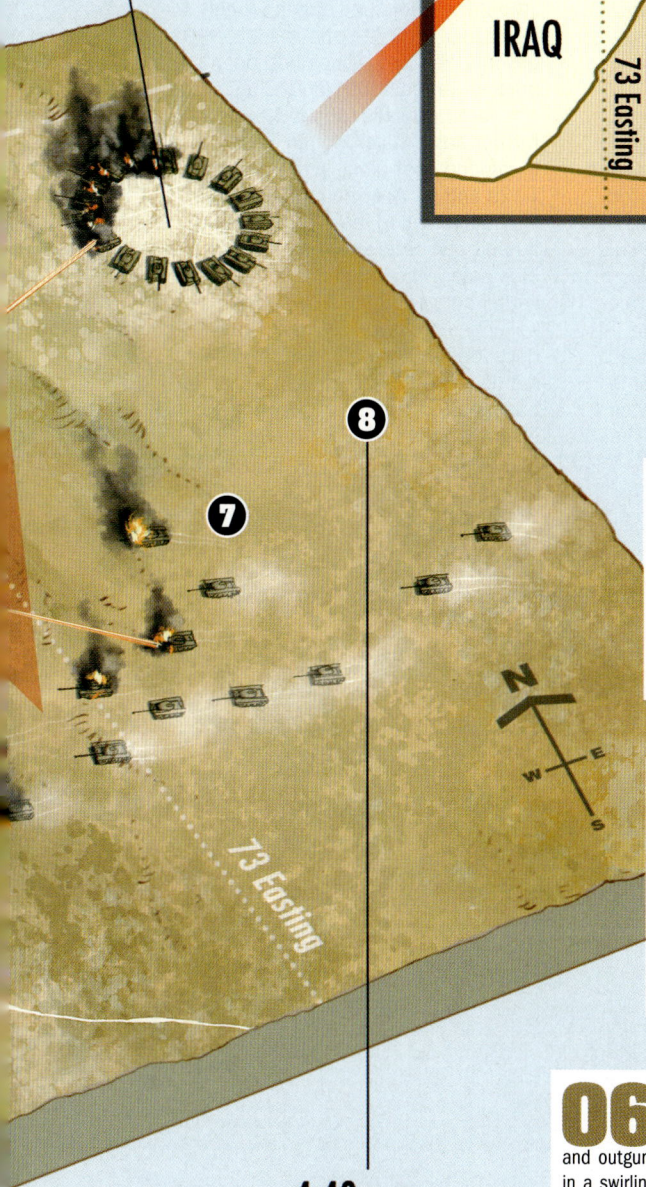

IRAQ

KUWAIT

73 Easting

Armored vehicle
US M1A1 Tank
Iraqi Tank

8

7

N
W    E
S

73 Easting

**04 CHANCE ENCOUNTER**

Eagle Troop, 2nd ACR detects prepared Iraqi defensive positions as one of its Bradley CFVs rolls atop an enemy bunker and at least 40 T-72 and T-55 tanks are observed dug in on the reverse slope of a low ridge.

**05 PUSHING FORWARD**

Advancing toward 70 Easting, Eagle Troop and other elements of 2nd ACR engage dozens of Iraqi tanks and armoured vehicles. The M1A1 Abrams of troop commander Captain HR McMaster takes out three Iraqi tanks in eight seconds.

**06 WITHOUT ORDERS**

2nd ACR, outnumbered and outgunned, becomes embroiled in a swirling fight. Unable to extricate Eagle Troop from contact, McMaster advances beyond 70 Easting, his prescribed limit of advance.

4:40 p.m.
McMaster
halts troops

**08 1ST DIVISION FORWARD**

Having engaged well beyond its initial mission instructions, 2nd ACR stands aside as the heavy tank and armoured units of the 1st Infantry Division pass through their positions en route to Objective Norfolk and further attrition of Iraqi armoured forces.

**07 73 EASTING SLEDGEHAMMER**

In just over 20 minutes, the Abrams tanks and Bradley CFVs of 2nd ACR destroy 28 Iraqi tanks and more than 40 other enemy vehicles, expending large amounts of ammunition and TOW anti-tank missiles.

operations and phoney radio traffic created the impression that the Coalition intended to invade Kuwait from the south, into the most formidable Iraqi defences, Schwarzkopf directed a massive force of several combat divisions to sweep westward in a wide arc, taking up positions to attack to the north and northeast into Iraq in a wide envelopment.

Air bombardment had succeeded in effectively blinding the Iraqi high command, maximising the effectiveness of the southern deception such that the bulk of the enemy forces were oriented toward the coastline in anticipation of an amphibious landing. Meanwhile, the four divisions of the XVIII Airborne Corps, the US 82nd and 101st Airborne Divisions, US 24th Infantry Division (Mechanized) and the French 6th Light Division established flank security for the sledgehammer of the US VII Corps. The US VII Corps comprised of the US 1st and 3rd Armored Divisions, 1st Infantry Division and 1st Cavalry Division, along with the British 1st Armoured Division churning from its jump-off points in Saudi Arabia and racing to cut off the retreat of Iraqi forces once the enemy realised that the major threat was to its rear.

The culmination of Operation Desert Sabre, the ground component of Desert Storm, was a stunning victory over the Iraqi forces. Schwarzkopf explained: "Once we had taken out his eyes, we did what could best be described as the 'Hail Mary' play in football. This was absolutely an extraordinary move. I must tell you I can't recall any time in the annals of military history when this number of forces have moved over this distance to put themselves in a position to be able to attack. I think it was pretty effective."

The electrifying advance of VII Corps during the 100 hours of the ground war was punctuated by sharp clashes between its superb M1A1 Abrams main battle tanks, with M3 Bradley cavalry fighting vehicles, and those of the Iraqi Republican Guard – Soviet-made T-72 tanks and older T-62 and T-55 models and BMP infantry fighting vehicles. At the tip of the VII Corps spear, the three squadrons of the

*The Iraqi forces' Soviet-built tanks were no match for the coalition's modern weaponry*

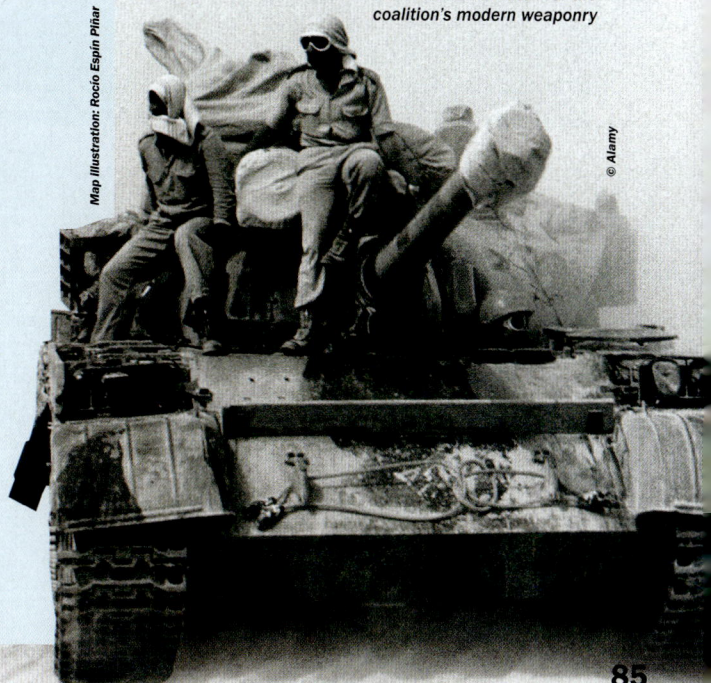

Map Illustration: Rocío Espín Piñar

© Alamy

US 2nd Armored Cavalry Regiment (2nd ACR) embarked on a covering force mission during the envelopment of the enemy forces in Kuwait. When the Iraqi senior commanders became aware of the 'Hail Mary' movement, the Republican Guard Tawakalna Mechanized Division was repositioned to the west to contest the advance of VII Corps.

On 26 February, the second full day of the ground war, the 2nd ACR ranged forward of the Coalition juggernaut to make contact with enemy forces to their front, determine their strength and find or create weak points before the bulk of the VII Corps armoured fist was brought to bear.

## The battle commences

As the 2nd ACR crossed the Iraqi frontier, it penetrated roughly 12.5 miles (20km) and encountered enemy resistance for the first time on the evening of 24 February. Bradleys responded with 1in (25mm) cannon fire and TOW wire-guided anti-tank missiles, while mortar rounds were fired effectively. Large numbers of Iraqi soldiers surrendered to the regiment's Fox (F) Troop that night. The following day, Ghost (G) Troop destroyed an Iraqi scout unit of 12 small armoured vehicles. Intelligence gleaned from the action indicated that the Republican Guard was in the vicinity, and orders were subsequently received for the planned turn from the northward penetration to a northeastern axis of advance.

After a night of heavy rain, elements of the 2nd ACR defeated several companies of the Iraqi 50th Brigade on 26 February and received orders to adjust the regiment's operational boundary with the British 1st Armoured Division to the south. An Iraqi tank was destroyed in the subsequent manoeuvre. By late morning a fierce sandstorm restricted visibility, but all three squadrons of the 2nd ACR engaged elements of the Tawakalna Division near 60 Easting, a location corresponding to map coordinates in the virtually featureless desert. By noon, the cavalrymen reported 23 Iraqi T-55s, 25 armoured personnel carriers and other vehicles destroyed.

The 2nd ACR was ordered to continue its advance to 70 Easting but to avoid bringing on a general engagement forward of VII Corps as the heavy combat formations proceeded on a front of four armoured and mechanised divisions. The three squadrons of the 2nd ACR advanced with eight of the regiment's nine cavalry troops abreast in search of the Republican Guard. Eagle (E) Troop of 2nd Squadron (Cougar Squadron) moved forward generally in a wedge formation, its strength 12 Bradley CFVs and nine M1A1s with their burly 4.7in (120mm) smoothbore guns. The Americans were unaware that they had entered an Iraqi training ground or that a road ran parallel and through a nearby village before proceeding across the Kuwaiti border.

Anticipating enemy contact, the Iraqi commander, a Major Mohammed who

had actually trained in the United States previously, had established defensive positions along the reverse slope of a slight ridge, hoping that any opposing tanks would crest the high ground and immediately become vulnerable as they topped the elevation. He also fortified the village with anti-aircraft guns to be used in an anti-personnel role along with troops and machine-gun positions to defend an approach along the road. According to Captain HR McMaster, commanding Eagle Troop, the Iraqis had dug in roughly 40 T-72s and 16 BMPs about 3,000ft (915m) beyond the ridge. Mines had been sown, and bunkers and defensive trenches screened the armoured vehicles. About 9,000ft (2,740m) further east, Major Mohammed placed his command post along with a reserve of 18 T-72s and other armoured vehicles.

As Eagle Troop reached 67 Easting, where it had been ordered to halt, fighting erupted. McMaster, who later rose to the rank of lieutenant general and served as national security advisor to President Donald Trump, described the contact: "Staff Sergeant John McReynolds' Bradley drove atop an Iraqi bunker serving as an observation post. Two enemy soldiers emerged and surrendered, and McReynolds took them to the rear. The Bradley of McReynolds' wingman, Sergeant Maurice Harris, came under fire. As Harris engaged the enemy with his 25mm, 1st Lieutenant Tim Gauthier fired a TOW missile into the village so the explosion would orient our tanks. After

*Abrams tanks from 3rd Armored Division during Operation Desert Storm, February 1991*

my gunner, Staff Sergeant Craig Koch, fired a round to mark the target centre, all nine tanks fired high-explosive rounds into the village to suppress the enemy position."

When Harris reported that enemy troops were firing at his Bradley, the response from his platoon leader was to the point: "Well, kill them!"

As Eagle Troop, the remainder of 2nd Squadron and 3rd Squadron fought the Iraqis at 67 Easting, McMaster received permission to move ahead to 70 Easting, and the fighting spread to the south and east. Unknown to the cavalrymen, they were outnumbered at least three to one. Another Bradley took out an Iraqi T-72 with a TOW missile, and E Troop shifted to a 'tanks forward' combat configuration. McMaster's tank, nicknamed Mad Max, rolled up a small hill north of the village, and Koch yelled: "Tanks direct front."

McMaster remembered: "From my hatch I could see eight T-72s in prepared positions directly to our front. As I sent a contact report to the troop, Koch destroyed two more tanks. Then all nine Abrams engaged together as we advanced. Within about a minute everything within the range of our guns was in flames."

In approximately eight seconds, Koch and Mad Max had destroyed three Iraqi T-72s. During the one-sided fight, the nine Abrams tanks of Eagle Troop had destroyed 28 Iraqi tanks, 16 armoured fighting vehicles and 30 trucks in just 23 minutes. There were no American casualties in that engagement.

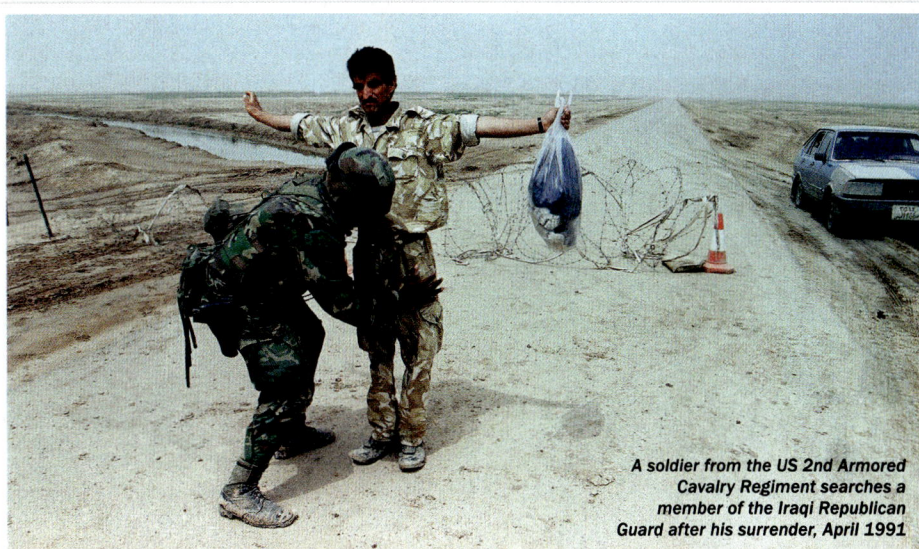

*A soldier from the US 2nd Armored Cavalry Regiment searches a member of the Iraqi Republican Guard after his surrender, April 1991*

While McMaster was fully involved in clearing the westernmost Iraqi defensive positions, Lieutenant John Gifford, his executive officer, chimed in on the radio: "I know you don't want to know this right now, but you're at the limit of advance; you're at the 70 Easting." McMaster quickly replied: "Tell them we can't stop. Tell them we're in contact, and we have to continue this attack. Tell them I'm sorry."

Despite the order to avoid a general engagement, Eagle Troop and the rest of 2nd ACR had run into a much larger enemy force and were unable to prevent the battle from steadily escalating. McMaster was compelled to stay in the fight and could not disengage to a defensive position. Although the original plan had been to locate the Republican Guard and then move aside to allow the heavy divisions of VII Corps to pass through and take on the enemy elite, McMaster's only alternative was to fight on, possibly preventing the larger VII Corps divisional forces' deployment from their road march formations to combat wedges with tanks forward. Then, there was also the

> ## "ALL NINE ABRAMS ENGAGED TOGETHER AS WE ADVANCED. WITHIN ABOUT A MINUTE EVERYTHING WITHIN THE RANGE OF OUR GUNS WAS IN FLAMES"

*In just over 20 minutes, 28 Iraqi tanks and over 40 other vehicles were destroyed*

possibility of the armoured cavalry squadrons being overwhelmed by a major counter-attack – but McMaster showed initiative as the situation dictated.

Pushing ahead, Eagle Troop was becoming fully engaged with the 18th Mechanized Battalion of the Tawakalna Division. The Battle of 73 Easting was steadily growing as other elements of the 2nd ACR continued their advance. The 1st and 3rd Troops, 2nd ACR, had fought the Iraqi 50th Armored Brigade the previous day and were now engaging the surviving elements of that unit as well as the 37th Brigade of the Iraqi 12th Armored Division south of the Tawakalna Division positions. Iron (I) Troop, 3rd Squadron, filled a gap in the line of advance, while Ghost Troop, 2nd Squadron, north of Eagle Troop, and Killer (K) Troop, 3rd Squadron pitched in. Fighting raged as the Sun set and the desert was shrouded in darkness.

McMaster directed Eagle Troop to 73 Easting, the ridgeline where the Iraqi tank reserve was located. "My tank and others destroyed the first of the reserve from a range of approximately 1,000 yards [914m] beginning at about 1640," he recalled. "We could not see the others until we crested the rise and entered the assembly area. The enemy reserve was attempting to move out, but E Troop tanks destroyed all of them at close range before they could deploy."

Meanwhile, Iron Troop fought its way to 70 Easting and destroyed 16 Iraqi tanks with early support from Killer Troop. Advancing through the blazing hulks of enemy armoured

## "WE WERE ABLE TO OBLITERATE THE IRAQI T-72 AND T-55 TANK FORCE BECAUSE THE IRAQIS WERE ABYSMALLY PREPARED"

vehicles, Iron Troop destroyed an enemy battalion command post.

Elsewhere, Ghost Troop took up positions on a low ridgeline and fought off counter-attacks by tanks of the Tawakalna and 12th Armored Divisions for several hours. Waves of infantry streamed alongside the Iraqi tanks, threatening to overrun the Americans. Air support had been spotty at best due to the inclement weather, but it provided great assistance along with concentrated artillery fire in beating back the attackers. By 9pm, Ghost Troop had fired more than half its available TOW missiles, and artillery and MLRS rocket systems had fired more than 700 rounds in support. By the time the Iraqi attacks petered out, Ghost Troop had destroyed two companies of enemy tanks and inflicted scores of casualties, the bodies of Iraqi soldiers strewn across the desert floor.

Eagle Troop fought off occasional infantry attacks and took on a company-size counter-attack by T-72s and BMPs at long range, destroying the enemy armoured vehicles before they could engage. "The mortar section

suppressed enemy infantry farther east, and two artillery strikes devastated enemy logistical bases," recalled McMaster. "First Sergeant Bill Virrill led a team to clear bunkers using grenades and satchel charges. Just after 2200 the 1st Infantry Division moved forward through the Allied front line in 3rd Squadron's sector to E Troop's south."

During the melee the 2nd ACR front extended to 74 Easting, and the 1st Infantry Division began passing through the cavalry lines in darkness around 2am on February 27. Its immediate attention was focused on Objective Norfolk, the intersection of the main road into Kuwait and several dusty desert trails. What was left of the 18th Mechanized and 37th Brigades was now up against more than a handful of Abrams and Bradleys, which had already taken the measure of them. The vanguard of the 1st Infantry Division included six battalions of M1A1 tanks, well over 300 in total, backed by heavy 6in (155mm) field artillery and air support as the weather improved.

Task Force 1-41, a brigade-sized force that was the first US combat formation to pierce the Iraqi line of defences and operate in enemy territory back on 15 February, encountered a battalion of enemy T-55 tanks, some of which had not turned their engines over and did not present a signature to thermal imaging equipment. A Bradley unit became disoriented and passed in front of enemy positions, taking fire that destroyed a single cavalry fighting vehicle and killed the three American crewmen.

The Abrams' 4.7in (120mm) smoothbore gun could knock out enemy armour from a distance of 8,200ft (2,500m)

American troops from 2nd ACR examine the cockpit of a destroyed MiG-23 jet fighter, April 1991

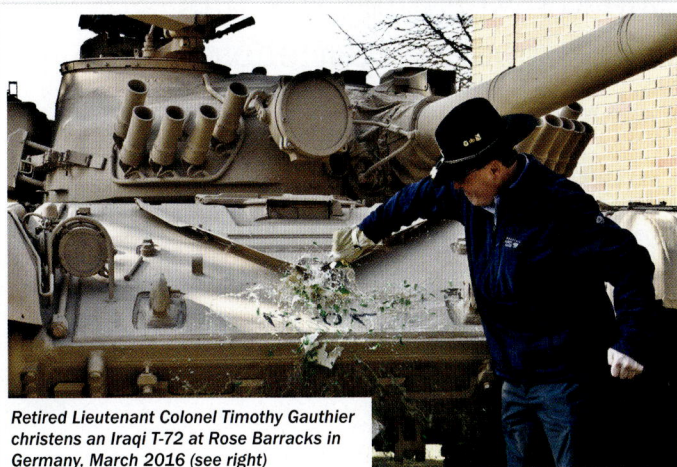

Retired Lieutenant Colonel Timothy Gauthier christens an Iraqi T-72 at Rose Barracks in Germany, March 2016 (see right)

In March 2016 2nd ACR held a ceremony at Rose Barracks to mark 25 years since the Battle of 73 Easting

After the initial enemy fire was detected, a company of M1A1s blasted three of the Iraqi tanks before they were able to reload and fire their main 3.9in (100mm) rifled cannon a second time. An incident of friendly fire followed when several other M1A1s opened fire, hitting three more Bradleys. The Task Force 1-41 commander consolidated his position and ordered an artillery bombardment to break up Iraqi infantry attacks and dislodge enemy armour.

Within hours Task 1-41 would spearhead the US drive on Objective Norfolk, where another armoured engagement occurred. At times, the Iraqis stood and fought. However, on many occasions they chose to surrender. Either way, the outcome of the mighty coalition ground assault in Operation Desert Storm was inevitable.

## Aftermath

During the Battle of 73 Easting, American forces suffered only six casualties. A Bradley of Ghost Troop was out of action as its 1in (25mm) cannon had jammed and its TOW launcher was not operating. While the crew attempted to clear the cannon, an Iraqi BMP, which was thought to have been silenced, fired a 2.9in (73mm) shell that struck the Bradley and killed Sergeant Nels Moller. Other casualties inflicted during continuation actions were caused primarily by friendly fire. One M1A1 was slightly damaged by a mine, and a single Bradley was lost to enemy action at 73 Easting itself.

In sharp contrast, the 2nd Armored Cavalry Regiment, outnumbered significantly, had shown outstanding tactical manoeuvre and combat initiative among its line officers in the destruction of the 18th Mechanized and 37th Brigades of the Iraqi Tawakalna and 12th Armored Divisions respectively. The 2nd and 3rd Squadrons, 2nd ACR destroyed an estimated 159 Iraqi tanks and more than 250 other vehicles, inflicting as many as 1,000 casualties on the enemy and taking approximately 2,000 prisoners. The 2nd Squadron accounted for 55 enemy tanks and 45 other vehicles.

Retired Colonel Daniel L Davis, who fought in the Battle of 73 Easting as a lieutenant, commented: "We were able to devastate the Iraqi T-72s during the Battle of 73 Easting for two compounding reasons. First, we as a squadron and regiment had trained exhaustively for more than a year prior to Saddam Hussein invading Kuwait in August 1990, and then stepped up another level from November when we were alerted for deployment through February shortly before we began the attack… Secondly, we were able to obliterate the Iraqi T-72 and T-55 tank force because the Iraqis were abysmally prepared."

The Battle of 73 Easting is remembered as one of the largest armoured battles in the history of the US armed forces and one of the last such engagements of the 20th century. At 73 Easting and elsewhere, coalition forces demonstrated superior training, tactical coordination and technical prowess. While the American and British armoured units fielded tanks and other weapons systems that employed the latest in technological advancements, including superior optics and target acquisition equipment, the Iraqi enemy generally operated Soviet-built export models of the T-72 and main battle tanks that were at least a generation behind in their battlefield capability.

The Battle of 73 Easting established coalition forces as disciplined, well-trained, capably led and equipped with the latest in land warfare weaponry and systems. Although its employment was somewhat dictated by adverse weather, air superiority played a key role from the inception of Operation Desert Storm, through 73 Easting and to the conclusion of the 100-hour ground war that ejected the Iraqi Army from Kuwait, shattered the elite Republican Guard and inflicted a stinging defeat on the forces of Saddam Hussein.

## FURTHER READING

- The Editors of *Military History Magazine*, *Desert Storm* (Empire Press, 1991)
- Andrew Leyden, *An After Action Report: Gulf War Debriefing Book* (Hellgate Press, 1997)
- Douglas Macgregor, *Warrior's Rage: The Great Tank Battle of 73 Easting* (Naval Institute Press, 2009)
- Brigadier General Robert H Scales, *Certain Victory: The U.S. Army in the Gulf War* (Brassey's, 1994)

Images: Alamy, Getty

# M1 ABRAMS
## MAIN BATTLE TANK

### Since its debut in the 1980s, the M1 Abrams tank has maintained a combat edge on the modern battlefield

**WORDS: MICHAEL E. HASKEW**

In the mid-1970s, the lengthy MBT-70 joint venture between the United States and the Federal Republic of Germany to produce a main battle tank collapsed due to divergent priorities with the developing weapons system. As a result, each country then pursued its own programme. In the United States, the result was the prototype XM-1, which was delivered to the US Army for field evaluation in 1976.

By 1978, Chrysler Corporation initiated production, and two years later the first operational M1 Abrams third-generation main battle tank entered service, a contemporary of the German Leopard 2 main battle tank. A total of 3,273 M1 tanks were built for the US, introducing to the American arsenal a modern armoured vehicle replacing the latest in the Patton tank series,

which had served since the 1950s. The M1 had modern features such as the multi-fuel gas turbine engine and Chobham composite armour, along with computer fire control, NBC (nuclear, biological, chemical) protection as well as separate ammunition storage in a blowout compartment that enhanced crew survivability in the event of a catastrophic explosion.

During more than 40 years of service, the M1, named for US General Creighton Abrams, has proven itself, with major upgrades, to be a lethal presence on the battlefield. Major improvement programmes have led to significant model revisions, including the M1A1 in 1985, the M1A2 in 1996, the current M1A2 SEPv3 enhancement programme, as well as the M1E3 upgrade that is expected to extend the service life of the Abrams into the year 2040

### MAIN ARMAMENT

The Rheinmetall L44 4.7in (120mm) smoothbore gun replaced an original British-designed 4.1in (105mm) main weapon in upgraded versions of the M1 Abrams main battle tank. It's capable of firing the advanced M829A4 (AMP) multi-purpose ammunition round. The weapon is manually loaded from within the turret, stabilised in two planes and accurate for firing on the move.

*Below: An M1 Abrams main battle tank crosses the River Euphrates during the Iraq War in 2003*

### HULL ARMOUR

A third-generation composite armour, based on the original revolutionary Chobham, includes plates of depleted uranium and provides protection against enemy projectiles that equals roughly 38in (965mm) of rolled homogeneous steel. The improved armour provides greater protection and survivability for the crew.

Images: Getty, Wiki / PD / Gow

and perhaps beyond. Well over 10,000 Abrams tanks in all variants have been produced in the last half-century, and ttanks from the M1 series have been purchased by or entered service with at least ten countries.

The impressive combat record of the M1 and successor Abrams variants includes Gulf War of 1991, the 'Global War on Terror' (specifically in Iraq and Afghanistan), the Iraq War and other deployments. It has demonstrated significant prowess against tanks constructed during the Soviet era.

*M1 Abrams main battle tanks manoeuvre during exercises in Operation Reforger, 1985*

## SECONDARY ARMAMENT

The 0.5in (12.7mm) M2HB heavy machine gun is turret-mounted aboard the M1 Abrams tank series and represents a modernisation of the fabled M2 .50-calibre machine gun developed by John Browning. A pair of .30-calibre machine guns provides close support against infantry attack or allows the tank to add small-arms fire in an assault.

## TURRET

The characteristic low-profile turret of the M1 Abrams tank series contributes to an overall minimal silhouette for the vehicle and houses three of the tank's four crewmen: gunner, loader and commander. The turret is further configured to accommodate the breech of the main 4.7in (120mm) weapon and technology for target acquisition, navigation and sophisticated armour protection.

> "WELL OVER 10,000 ABRAMS TANKS IN ALL VARIANTS HAVE BEEN PRODUCED"

## M1A2 ABRAMS
## MAIN BATTLE TANK

| | |
|---|---|
| COMMISSIONED | 1996 |
| ORIGIN | USA |
| LENGTH | 32FT, 3IN (9.83M) |
| RANGE | 265 MILES (426KM)) |
| ENGINE | HONEYWELL AGT 1500 GAS TURBINE POWERPLANT DESIGNED BY LYCOMING TEXTRON GENERATING 1,118KW, OR 1,520 HORSEPOWER |
| CREW | 4 |
| ARMOUR | COMPOSITE APPLIQUÉ ARMOUR WITH EQUIVALENT PROTECTION ESTIMATED UP TO 37.7 IN (960MM) OF HOMOGENOUS ROLLED STEEL |
| PRIMARY WEAPON | 1 X 4.7IN (120MM) M256 SMOOTHBORE GUN |
| SECONDARY WEAPON | 2 X 0.3IN (7.62MM) M240 MACHINE GUNS; 1 X 0.5IN (12.7MM) M2HB MACHINE GUN |

*Illustration: Nicholas Forder*

49035013

350 4 4

## POWERPLANT

The Honeywell AGT1500 gas turbine engine installed with the M1 Abrams tank series was a great leap forward in armoured vehicle propulsion. The multi-fuel engine generates 1,500hp, a top speed of 42mph (68kp/h) and tremendous acceleration. Nicknamed 'Whispering Death,' the engine is noted for quiet running.

# ARMAMENT

Early Abrams tanks mounted a main armament of the 4.1in (105mm) M68 A1 rifled gun, constructed on a British Royal Ordnance design. With the M1A1, the primary weapon was replaced by the 4.7in (120mm) M256 smoothbore gun adapted from the German Rheinmetall L44 weapon and built under licence. The M256 is capable of firing an array of ordnance, including the M829A4 advanced multi-purpose (AMP) round. Experiments with the longer 4.7in (120mm) L55 have likely resulted in maintaining the L44 as the M1 series primary weapon. Secondary .30-calibre and .50 calibre machine guns provide defence against infantry and lower level air attack.

*Right: The 4.7in (120mm) smoothbore M256 main weapon mounted by the M1A1 Abrams is prominent in this photo of a Marine tank off-loading*

## "THE M256 IS CAPABLE OF FIRING AN ARRAY OF ORDNANCE, INCLUDING THE M829A4 ADVANCED MULTI-PURPOSE (AMP) ROUND"

*Below: US Army M1 Abrams manoeuvre into firing positions during Operation Reforger, 1985*

*Above: An Australian soldier is alert adjacent to the turret-mounted .50-calibre M2HB machine gun aboard an Abrams tank, 2021*

*An M1A1 Abrams tank fires its M256 main weapon, a licence-built version of the German Rheinmetall L44*

*This M1A1 Abrams photographed in the field in 2007 exhibits the characteristic low profile and features of the TUSK urban enhancement package*

*M1A1 Abrams main battle tanks of the 3rd Armored Division move out on a mission during Operation Desert Storm*

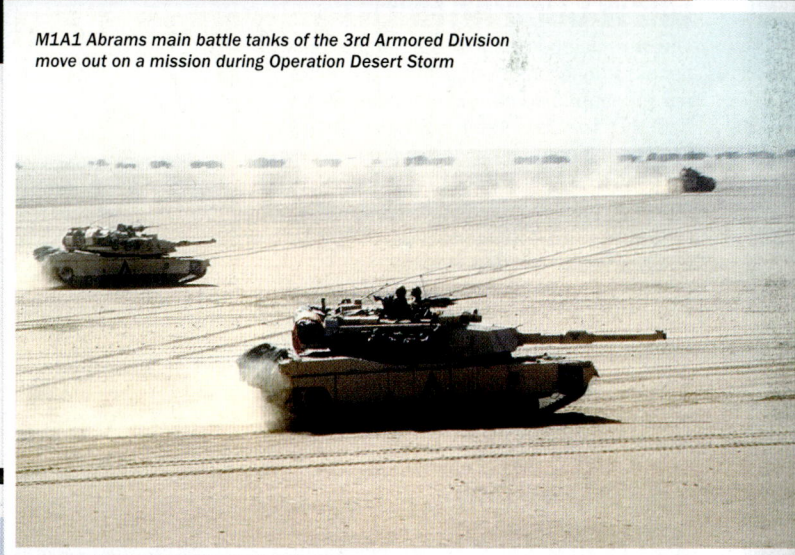

# DESIGN

The Abrams main battle tank series was designed to provide the most capable and robust armoured vehicle platform in the world in both offensive and defensive roles, particularly in the event of war in Europe with the Soviet Union and Warsaw Pact countries. Enhanced crew survivability was complemented in the original design with modern features. The design itself was intended to present a low profile, maximise the enhanced armour protection incorporated, and allow newly introduced target acquisition systems to operate with efficiency. More than a dozen upgrades were applied to the M1A1 alone, including the Tank Urban Survival Kit series (TUSK) that allowed greater security and proficiency in close-quarter urban environments.

*A Honeywell AGT 1500 gas turbine engine is eased into the engine compartment of an Abrams tank in Kuwait*

# ENGINES

With the introduction of the M1 Abrams, the US military broke the tradition of the diesel engines that had powered its armoured forces for decades. The Honeywell AGT 1,500-horsepower gas turbine engine, designed and built by Lycoming Textron, has earned a reputation for reliability in varied environmental conditions such as the temperature extremes of desert warfare, and its multi-fuel powerplant makes considerably less noise than its diesel predecessors. Providing an exceptional surge of power as needed, the gas turbine enables the Abrams to reach optimal cruising speed in a matter of seconds and rapidly hit a top speed of 42mph (68kp/h).

*Left: Tankers of the US 3rd Infantry Division man the gunner's and commander's positions in the turret of the M1A1 Abrams tank*

*Below: A destroyed Iraqi tank burns after the Battle of 73 Easting during the 1991 Gulf War*

# CREW COMPARTMENT

The crew compartment of the Abrams tank series is configured for optimal freedom of movement and comfort in the confines of both the chassis and turret. The internal layout positions the driver forward in a reclining seat that enables reduction of the tank's silhouette, while three adaptable periscopes facilitate operations at night and in adverse weather conditions. The three-man turret houses the gunner, seated to the right and utilising laser range-finding equipment, along with the loader, positioned to the left with clear access to the main weapon breech. The commander is seated to the right with a view of the battlefield through six periscopes.

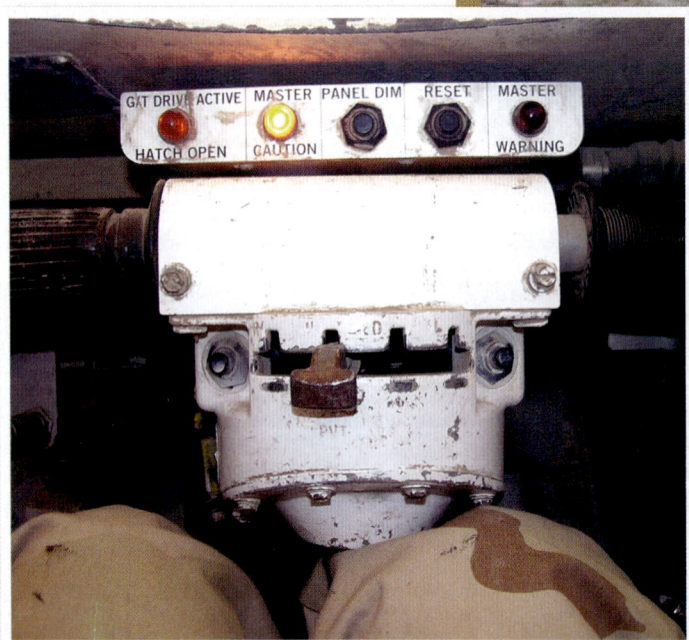

*Above: Components of the driving controls aboard the M1 Abrams tank series are seen in the driver's position in the tank's hull*

# SERVICE HISTORY

The US government approved the enhancement of 1,000 tanks to the M1A2 standard in 1996. The upgrade, performed at Lima Army Tank Plant in Ohio, validated the long-term investment in the Abrams. That investment had been justified to a great extent by the combat performance of the M1 series during the Gulf War of 1991. Although 14 Abrams tanks were damaged and nine destroyed during the Gulf War, none were lost to enemy tank fire. Seven were destroyed in incidents of friendly fire, and two intentionally to prevent capture by hostile forces.

In tank versus tank combat, the Abrams was clearly superior to the Soviet-made T-72, T-62 and T-54/55 tanks deployed by Iraqi forces. A total of 1,848 M1A1 tanks were deployed to Saudi Arabia during Operation Desert Storm.

The most famous Abrams performance during the Gulf War on occurred at the Battle of 73 Easting and a follow-up action at Objective Norfolk, 26-27 February 1991. At 73 Easting, four troops of the US 2nd Armored Cavalry Regiment destroyed two brigades of the Iraqi Tawakalna Division. Nine M1A1 Abrams tanks, accompanied by a dozen Bradley fighting vehicles, blasted dozens of enemy tanks and armoured vehicles. Only one Bradley was lost to hostile fire. After two days' combat, over 200 Iraqi armoured vehicles had been destroyed.

Later, performance in the Iraq War further burnished the Abrams's reputation. In the autumn of 2023, the US Army announced the M1E3 modernisation programme, which is expected to further increase the system's longevity.

*A US Army M1/A1 Abrams tank equipped with a mine plow participates in task force manoeuvres near the Iraqi border in the Kuwaiti desert, 16 December 2002*

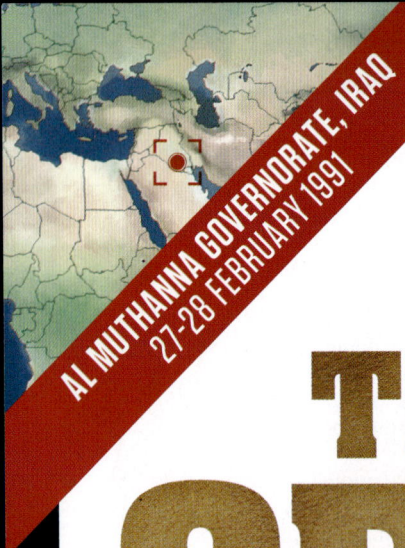

## Great Battles

# THE BATTLE OF OBJECTIVE NORFOLK

One of the largest tank fights of the Iraq War will be forever known to those who were there as "Fright Night"

**WORDS: BEN GAZUR**

The Iraqi authorities were certain that the Coalition attack would come directly into the Kuwaiti territory that Saddam Hussein's forces had captured. American ships were anchored in the bay beside the occupied Kuwaiti capital city. Iraqi armour and infantry were drawn up so as to hold the line in Kuwait against possible invasion of Kuwait. American air force pilots had spent January of 1991 pounding the artillery and military bases Iraq had set up and all seemed set for a battle in Kuwait. No one would be foolish enough to attack through the featureless and trackless desert west of Kuwait. Even the Iraqi military, trained on this terrain, would get hopelessly lost in this territory. General Norman Schwarzkopf, commander of Coalition forces, had other ideas however.

Indeed there would be a campaign aimed directly at Kuwait City, but there would be another attack taking place at the exact same time. The border between Iraq and Saudi Arabia was relatively weakly fortified as Iraqi command was preparing to defend Kuwait from assault. Instead of striking directly into Kuwait, and having to breach Iraqi defences there, Schwarzkopf planned a "left hook" attack using the American VII Corps. The Coalition forces would cross the Iraqi-Saudi border west of Kuwait and advance north before swinging eastwards to capture Kuwait City.

The burning of Kuwaiti oilfields produced a greasy fog which reduced visibility for both sides during the Battle of Norfolk

# OPPOSING FORCES

| IRAQI FORCES | VS | COALITION FORCES |
|---|---|---|
| **LEADERS** | | **LEADERS** |
| Salah Aboud Mahmoud, Saheb Mohammed Alaw | | Norman Schwarzkopf, Frederick Franks, Rupert Smith |
| **INFANTRY** | | **INFANTRY** |
| 9,000+ men | | VII Corps. 143,000 men. (Not all engaged) |
| **TANKS** | | **TANKS** |
| 900 | | 1487 (Not all engaged) |

*During the Battle of Norfolk exploding Iraqi tanks and transports created a hazardous rain of debris for infantry soldiers*

*The 105mm shells used by Abrams tanks proved capable of tearing through the armour of Iraqi tanks and caused devastating damage*

*A British Challenger tank destroyed an Iraqi tank at a distance of 5km – the longest tank-on-tank kill in military history*

This would bypass most of the Iraqi army and allow the Coalition forces to encircle and crush them. American reports in the media had helped to strengthen the impression that the main aim of their assault would come through Kuwait. Journalists were briefed on the tank battalions and infantry forces on the Kuwait border but the presence of large forces in the Saudi desert was not mentioned.

The Iraqi army was not entirely unprepared for the battle to come. They had at their disposal thousands of T-72 tanks which had been purchased from the Soviet Union. The designs for these tanks were around 20 years old by the time of the Gulf War but many had been constructed in Iraq with modifications to make them suitable for use in desert warfare. The Lion of Babylon tanks were modified T-72 that were given to the elite Republican Guard of the Iraqi army. Armed with a 125mm main gun there were fears among the coalition commanders that the T-72s would be able to cripple their tanks, especially given their large numerical superiority. The Iraqis could also call on even older Soviet era tanks.

The American forces mainly relied on M1A1 Abrams tanks which bore a 120mm main gun. These tanks had never seen use in combat and there was the possibility that they would prove to have drawbacks against the older T-72s. The Abrams was a behemoth of a machine and weighed over 60 tons which

made it one of the heaviest tanks constructed. Would they be able to move effectively in the desert? The British 1st Armoured Division, using Challenger tanks, was set to guard the right flank during the advance. Both were supported by armoured people carriers and self-propelling artillery.

American and British artillery softened the ground for the invasion by bombarding Iraqi positions with over 90,000 rounds. These attacks, reinforced by air raids, essentially wiped out all Iraqi long range attacks. On 24 January, Operation Desert Sabre, the ground invasion of Iraq, began. Coalition forces had to break through trenches and faced Iraqi tanks which had been dug in to offer them better protection from Coalition fire. Large numbers of Iraqi infantry fought back with small arms fire and swarmed Coalition armour – though with no ability to penetrate it. The breach into Iraq was made and the army was ordered to move to Objective Norfolk, a position in the desert which would disrupt Iraqi supply and defence lines and capture a supply depot. Around 1,500 coalition tanks moved forward towards 1,400 Iraqi tanks.

Conditions for the advance were literally hazy. As well as the usual fog of war the air was filled with the oily soot produced by the infernos in the Kuwaiti oilfields. Then a rain began to fall which reduced visibility further and turned the ground to a thick mud.The

Battle of Norfolk took place in the aftermath of the fight at 73 Easting 12km from Objective Norfolk. The Iraqi commanders had already seen how the Coalition forces were able to scatter Iraqi formations, especially those made up of sometimes unwilling conscripts. The Republican Guard were the best of Saddam Hussein's army, loyal and well supplied. It was feared they would fight to the death for their leader. They had been moved into position when it was realised that the Coalition was attempting to flank the Iraqi position in Kuwait.

The attack on Objective Norfolk began at just after midnight on 27 February. The Battle of 73 Easting had brought Coalition forces close to Norfolk but Iraqi defences and armed strength presented a formidable obstacle to advance. In the midst of rain, smoke, and darkness those on the Coalition side described how all they could hear was the roar of the tanks coming out of the gloom.

Fighting in darkness is always a dangerous affair and historically was the reason that most battles took place during the day. The commanders of the Coalition forces were not throwing their men into a blind battle though because of the advanced night vision technology that they were equipped with. Thermal images revealed the locations of Iraqi encampments and the tanks ranged against them. Each soldier might have been unable to see the enemy but they were able to pick them out through their screens. The horizon was dotted with Iraqi emplacements.

The Iraqi forces in turn had absolutely no idea of the large force which was preparing to attack. The Coalition forces were able to call on the first generation of GPS tracking devices which used satellites to pinpoint their positions. Despite this there were errors in maintaining the planned attack formations. Some platoons became disorientated in the dark and many were heavily sleep-deprived having come directly from the battle at 73 Easting. These mistakes sometimes put Coalition forces in harm's way.

The Iraqis were huddled in the night to protect themselves from potential air assault. Those manning tanks could not visualise the Coalition forces as they lacked any advanced night vision and could only have spotted them if they came close enough to be lit up by floodlights. The only other source of light were the fires from already burning Iraqi tanks. Veterans of the battle recall that these did present a danger as moving too close to them made you a very tempting target.

Advancing towards Objective Norfolk a Bradley platoon of infantry in armoured vehicles was caught in the glare of one of these fires while advancing behind some Abrams tanks. They had thought that the burning tanks were all that remained of Iraqi tanks in the area, not noticing that there were still five Iraqi T-55 tanks dug in and hidden by walls of earth. These were almost invisible with their engines turned off. When the Iraqis spotted the Americans they opened fire and destroyed one Bradley vehicle and killed three soldiers within it.

The Americans fought back. The firefight between the American infantry and the Iraqi tanks alerted a force of Abrams tanks behind

## 06 FRIGHT NIGHT

The darkness causes difficulties in holding formation for the Coalition forces. Advancing American tanks sometimes find themselves fired on by Iraqi tanks that had been hidden. Iraqi rounds do little against Abrams tanks – but friendly fire causes several deaths.

## 01 BATTLE OF NORFOLK

At 00:30 on February 27 VII Corps, with the British 1st Armoured Division protecting its right flank, move to capture Objective Norfolk. They are met with resistance from members of the Iraqi Republican Guard using T-72 tanks and infantry mounted anti-armour weaponry.

## 02 LEFT HOOK

Operation Desert Sabre was the planned ground invasion of Iraq by coalition forces. After advancing north into Iraq the army would swing eastwards to envelop Iraqi forces and cut off their retreat from Kuwait.

## 03 TASK FORCE IRON

The spearhead of the American advance is formed of Task Force 1-41 Infantry, who perform breaching manoeuvres and raids against Iraqi positions. They play a vital role in clearing trenches, bunkers, and other targets.

OBJ COLLINS

3-5
4-7
1-4
2-2ACR
1-34
5-16
2-34
4-37
3-37

3AD
XX
1ID

1
XX
3-2AD

# FIRST INFANTRY DIVISION OBJECTIVE NORFOLK

## OPERATION DESERT STORM
## 26-27TH FEBRUARY 1991

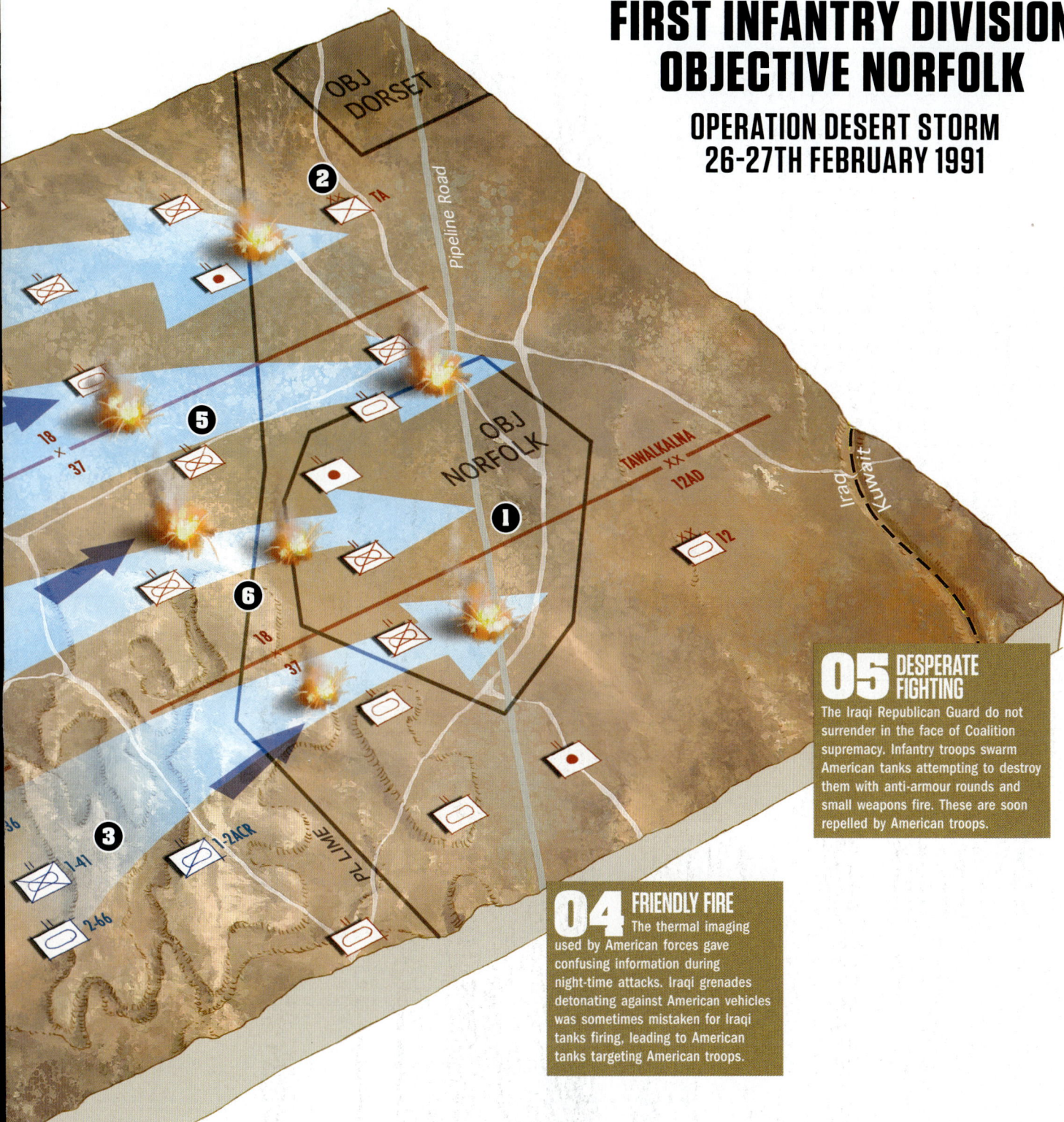

OBJ DORSET

**2**

TA

Pipeline Road

**5**

18

37

OBJ NORFOLK

TAWALKALNA

XX

12AD

**1**

**6**

18

37

XX 12

Iraq

Kuwait

**05 DESPERATE FIGHTING**

The Iraqi Republican Guard do not surrender in the face of Coalition supremacy. Infantry troops swarm American tanks attempting to destroy them with anti-armour rounds and small weapons fire. These are soon repelled by American troops.

36

**3**

1-2ACR

PL LIME

1-41

2-66

**04 FRIENDLY FIRE**

The thermal imaging used by American forces gave confusing information during night-time attacks. Iraqi grenades detonating against American vehicles was sometimes mistaken for Iraqi tanks firing, leading to American tanks targeting American troops.

ARMOUR
ARMOURED CAVALRY
MECHANISED INFANTRY

ARMOUR
ARMOURED CAVALRY
MECHANISED INFANTRY
TOWED HOWITZER

Initial attacks by covering force

Follow-on main attacks by brigades

Map Illustration: Rocio Espin

*Tracer rounds lit the night sky at the Battle of Norfolk allowing a dim sense of the course of the fight as the coalition advanced*

*The Abrams tank was the backbone of the American armoured units which led the incursion into Iraq and fought at the Battle of Norfolk*

## "IT WAS FEARED THE REPUBLICAN GUARD WOULD FIGHT TO THE DEATH"

the infantry to the presence of Iraqi tanks and they joined the fight. Three of the Iraqi tanks were quickly obliterated but the flashes of light from the American infantry were also mistakenly identified as coming from Iraqi tanks. American anti-tank rounds found the Bradleys and destroyed three of them in a 'friendly fire' incident. The disarray of the Battle of Norfolk led to those who fought in it calling it "Fright Night".

When the attack order was given at 00:30 the Coalition forces began to fire rounds from their tanks and artillery at the Iraqi emplacements in front of Objective Norfolk. Taken entirely unaware the Iraqi troops had to rush from their bunkers and trenches to their tanks to attempt to get them into the fight.

The Iraqi infantry were also armed with rocket-propelled grenades (RPGs) and mortars that could rapidly be deployed against the enemy. Almost immediately confusion raged on the battlefield. This was not an orderly battle of a line of tanks firing in an orderly fashion against another line of tanks. Some sections moved faster than others. Some became lost and moved in advance of the enemy positions. Each group began having to fight a war coming at them from 360 degrees.

While the American tanks and troops were fitted with the most advanced night vision technology available at the time it was not always able to spot all Iraqi strongholds and bunkers. An armoured team might pass a seemingly empty point and find armour-piercing rounds being fired at them from the rear. The armour on an Abrams tank was most vulnerable at the back. Debate continues over whether hiding and attacking from the rear was an active Iraqi tactic to get closer to their opponents or whether it was simply taking opportunities as they occurred.

The nature of the fighting at the Battle of Norfolk makes it impossible to trace with any clarity the steps of the battle. In a sense each unit, each tank, and each soldier was engaged in their own fight that night. At any moment they might be engaged from any angle, and so the history of the battle has to be told as a series of vignettes from a multitude of perspectives instead.

Having to fight in multiple directions led to more friendly fire accidents. Some of these were drawn directly from the inability to tell who was a friend and who was a foe when so many rounds were being launched. Others were calculated risks. When one Coalition tank was targeted by an Iraqi soldier firing armour-piercing rounds a friendly tank opened fire with a machine gun to take him out. The bullets strafed the American tank, displeasing the commander inside, until it was pointed out that it was either leave them open to a close range attack or risk hitting them with small calibre rounds. When Iraqi infantry clambered around American tanks in search of a way to

Images: Alamy, Getty, Wikipedia

fire inside it became common for friendly tanks to spray each other with bullets to dislodge the enemies on them. Coalition forces started to fire on any enemy that was spotted, whether engaged or not, because of the risk of a seemingly abandoned tank firing on them.

It soon became apparent that the fear of Iraqi T-72s being any match for British or American tanks was unfounded. The main cannon of the Abrams tank could effectively fire at a target over 2.5km away, while the T-72 had a range a little under 2km. The Americans could open up while still safe from any returning fire – so long as they could spot the Iraqi forces first. The British Challenger tank managed even greater feats of accuracy when one scored the longest recorded tank kill after hitting a T-72 at a distance of nearly 5km. Even when struck directly by T-72 fire the Abrams proved highly resilient and only one was lost due to enemy action during the entire Gulf War. The only tanks capable of destroying Abrams or Challenger tanks were other Coalition tanks – making the danger of friendly fire far greater than the enemy.

When British and American tanks were struck by Iraqi fire from other tanks their advanced armour was able to deflect the majority of the damage. Firing armour-piercing rounds at the Iraqi tanks had devastating effects however. Coalition shells were able to break through not only the armour of the T-72 but also the piles of dirt which had been built up around them. In many cases the shell went through a bank of sand, through the tank, and out the other side.

Objective Norfolk was a centre of resupply for Iraqi forces in the area and so many of the vehicles which the Coalition forces encountered were full of munitions and fuel. When these were hit they often exploded violently. Infantry found themselves facing a rain of rounds which had been blasted into the air and shrouded in ever thicker smoke. This made it even harder to identify targets. Among the flaming wreckage of vehicles the burning bodies of the dead and dying could be seen with their fists curling upwards. Tracer fire criss-crossed the night sky, though fired from which side was hard to tell.

Bunkers and trenches had to be cleared to secure the passage of Coalition forces. Machine gun fire from tanks and infantry vehicles was poured into them, as well as explosives. Early battles with Iraqi forces had seen large numbers of the enemy quickly surrendering once coming under attack. That was not the experience during the Battle of Norfolk because the Coalition was facing units from the Republican Guard who fought to the death in many cases. They would emerge from their hiding places to fire on tanks and only stop when killed or wounded.

While the battle was being fought to capture Objective Norfolk, Coalition artillery to the rear continued to fire at targets far to the east. This covering fire prevented any Iraqi reinforcements arriving to solidify defences in the area. As it became clear that the Coalition forces had vast technical superiority over the enemy the following hours of the fighting were mainly concerned with with mopping up remaining pockets of resistance across the vast battlefield.

By the time dawn revealed a battlefield littered with corpses, shattered vehicles, and rising pillars of smoke, the Coalition had complete control of Objective Norfolk. The border road between Iraq and Saudi Arabia had been secured, and one of the largest support stations set up by Iraqi forces was either destroyed or taken.

There was to be no respite for the Coalition troops however. The left flank of the Republican Guard forces had been broken but now the army had to turn eastwards towards Kuwait and their final goal.

*Without the benefit of night vision and GPS tracking Coalition forces would have become lost during the night-time battle*

*In the aftermath of the Battle of Norfolk the Iraqi desert was littered with the burnt and burning wreckage of hundreds of Iraqi tanks*

## Aftermath

The Battle of Norfolk was in many ways not its own battle but just another stage in a rolling advance. The Iraqi forces which the Coalition faced were not really a unified opponent working in concert. The Iraqi military had imagined that their best hope of winning the Gulf War was to sink their units into the ground and make the invasion so costly in terms of men and materiel that the Coalition forces would accept a ceasefire. This calculation failed when the Iraqi forces proved to be no match for the Coalition troops and tanks. Because the Battle of Norfolk was part of a larger campaign it is impossible to give exact numbers of casualties sustained. Are losses just prior to the order to advance at 00:30 to be included as part of this battle? The best that can be given are estimations. The number of Iraqi tanks destroyed has been stated as between 550 and 700, which does not count the even larger number of other armoured vehicles. The Coalition forces lost four Abrams tanks, possibly due to friendly fire incidents. In terms of men the Coalition suffered 36 dead and 110 wounded while hundreds of Iraqi soldiers were killed, and thousands captured.

The speed of the advance surprised even Coalition leaders. The superiority of Coalition technology and armour was no doubt an advantage but in many cases the Iraqi army was in possession of equipment that could have inflicted damage to Coalition assets at a far greater rate than they actually did. Nor was the bravery of individual Iraqi soldiers lacking during the battle. It seems that while Coalition forces had benefited from intense training for a tank battle against Soviet armed forces, the Iraqi army had not been as well prepared for the fight which it was facing.

In the aftermath of the Battle of Norfolk there was no time for rest. The Coalition tanks and troops continued to travel deeper into Iraq, as well as swing east towards Kuwait. The resistance of the Iraqi military failed to cause any significant casualties or delay to the Coalition. Within days of the Battle of Norfolk the Iraqi army was in full retreat from its positions in Kuwait and streaming back across the border into Iraq. A ceasefire was signed soon afterwards, which concluded fighting less than 100 hours after the first Coalition tank had rolled into Iraq. 'Fright Night' was just one of many fights on the way to this victory, but it was one that no one who was there would ever be able to forget.

## "TAKEN ENTIRELY UNAWARE THE IRAQI TROOPS HAD TO RUSH FROM THEIR BUNKERS AND TRENCHES"

# THE HIGHWAY OF DEATH

## The Iraqi withdrawal from Kuwait turned into a chaotic rout, with thousands of vehicles and armour trapped and obliterated by the full force of the Coalition

**WORDS:** TIM WILLIAMSON

*A US burial detail tasked with burying dead Iraqi soldiers. The official number of dead has never been confirmed*

With Coalition forces sweeping away his occupation army in Kuwait, Saddam ordered his forces to withdraw back to Iraq on 25 February. However, extracting his beleaguered and embattled divisions would be no easy task – there was only one main route out of Kuwait and back into Iraq: Highway 80. Beginning in Kuwait City, the six-lane highway runs north for over 95km to the border, before continuing to Basra (as Highway 8 in Iraq).

As General Norman Schwarzkopf's 100,000-strong invasion pressed from the south and west, the Iraqi retreat turned into a rout, creating a desperate traffic jam on the northern highway. Coalition aircraft and ground forces targeted the the Iraqi columns relentlessly – on 26 February alone over 3,000 sorties were launched, mostly against targets stuck on what later became known as the Highway of Death. Everything from hulking B-52 bombers, to Harrier jets, A-10 warthogs and F-15E Strike Eagle jets joined the attack, launching air-to-ground missiles, dropping ordnance, or mowing down their targets with machine-gun fire.

Also joining the attack was the American carrier USS Ranger, which repositioned closer to the coast in order to bring its A-6 Intruder attack jets into closer range. These carrier aircraft were able to target convoys travelling an alternative north-east route along the Kuwaiti coast, inflicting heavy losses on the ground. It's estimated that at least 1,500 Iraqi tanks, trucks and APCs were obliterated on Highway 80, alongside scores of civilian cars, buses and trucks also fleeing the onslaught. "It was like shooting fish in a barrel," remarked one US pilot. In addition, several hundred vehicles were destroyed along the north-east coastal road. When journalists arrived at the scene, they found miles of burnt-out and mangled vehicles, along with the still smouldering remains of their occupants, many rendered unrecognisable as a result of the inferno. There remains no definitive number of those killed on the highway – the low estimate is of hundreds dead, with an unknown number managing to escape into the desert.

In a briefing at the White House on 27 February, Chairman of the Joint Chiefs of Staff Colin Powell reported the results of the Coalition success. "It's clear that the Iraqi army is broken," he told President George Bush. "If anything, they're just trying to get out." President Bush's advisers urged an end to the conflict, not only because the objective to end the Iraqi occupation had been met, but because they feared public outcry if the carnage on the Highway of Death were to be repeated. The attack on the highway remains one of the darkest and controversial events in the war.

*An Iraqi tank destroyed along the highway, with graffiti left by Coalition troops*

*Aerial view of Highway 80 in the aftermath of the US attack. Vehicles attempting to escape the inferno by veering into the desert were also caught and destroyed*

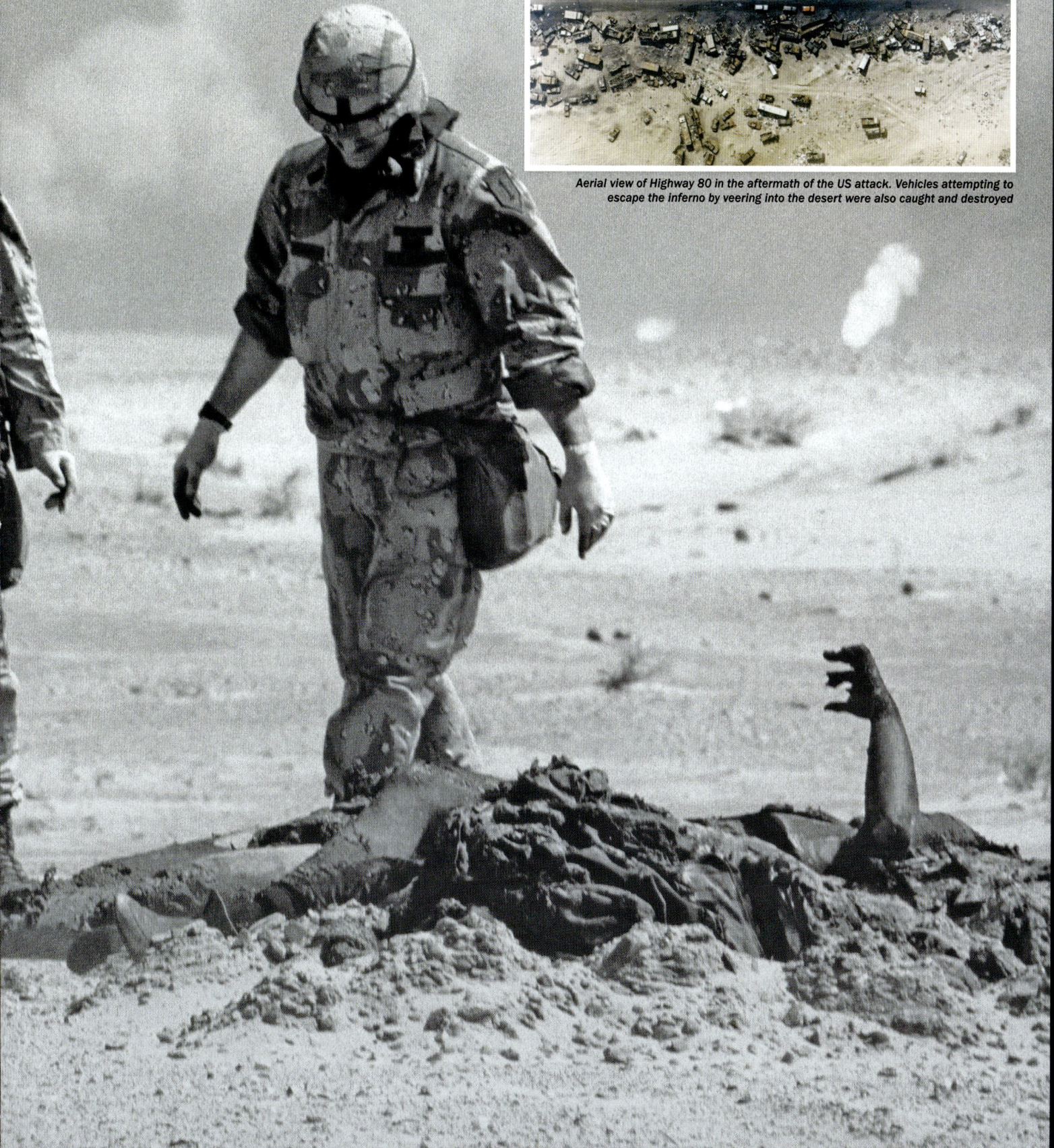

# BLACKBURN

With a distinguished career spanning several decades, the Buccaneer was one of the RAF's most effective strike jets

*Above: The Buccaneer was typically active in the North Sea area during its service*

**WORDS & IMAGES: NEILL WATSON**

Originally designed as a low-level strike and reconnaissance aircraft for carrier-borne operations, the Blackburn Buccaneer served on aircraft carriers with Britain's Fleet Air Arm for several years and was pressed into service with the Royal Air Force after the controversial cancellation of the TSR2 project.

The Buccaneer had a long service career, participating in all of the conflicts that British armed forces have been involved in until its retirement in 1994. At its high point, more than 100 Buccaneers served in the Royal Air Force. The aircraft was also supplied to the South African Air Force, where it was used for close air support in the Border Wars with Angola.

Following World War II, the Royal Navy became worried at the rapid expansion of the Soviet navy. The Russian introduction of very fast battle cruisers of similar design to the German pocket battleships of World War II was of great concern, as these new Soviet battleships were fast, highly manoeuvrable and would be a huge threat to Atlantic shipping in the event of an armed conflict. Rather than try to match the capability with expensive ship-building, in 1952 the decision was taken to design a fast, low-level strike aircraft capable of operating from aircraft carriers and delivering a large, sometimes nuclear, payload to strike against the Soviet navy.

## BLACKBURN BUCCANEER S2

**CREW:** 2 (PILOT AND OBSERVER)
**LENGTH:** 63FT 5IN (19.33M)
**WINGSPAN:** 44FT (13.41M)
**HEIGHT:** 16FT 3IN (4.97M)
**POWERPLANT:** 2 × ROLLS-ROYCE SPEY MK 101 TURBOFANS, 11,100LBF (49KN) EACH
**MAX SPEED:** 645MPH (560KN, 1,074KM/H) AT 200FT (60M)
**RANGE:** 2,300MI (2,000NMI, 3,700KM)
**HARDPOINTS:** 4 × UNDER-WING PYLON STATIONS, 1 × INTERNAL ROTATING BOMB BAY

WITH A CAPACITY OF 12,000LB (5,443KG) AND PROVISIONS TO CARRY COMBINATIONS OF:
**ROCKETS:** 4 × MATRA ROCKET PODS WITH 18 × SNEB 68MM ROCKETS EACH
**MISSILES:** 2 × AIM-9 SIDEWINDERS FOR SELF-DEFENCE OR 2 × AS-37 MARTEL MISSILES OR 4 × SEA EAGLE MISSILES
**BOMBS:** VARIOUS UNGUIDED BOMBS, LASER-GUIDED BOMBS, AS WELL AS THE RED BEARD OR WE.177 TACTICAL NUCLEAR BOMBS

*The Buccaneer was built to take off in the arduous maritime environment*

# BUCCANEER S2

Alamy

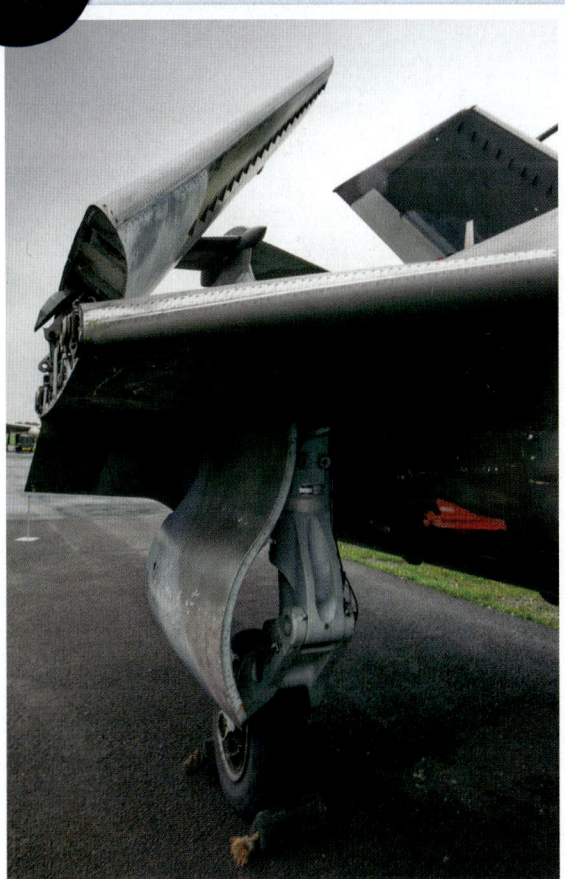

**Left:** Folding wings were part of the original Fleet Air Arm requirement

**Below:** The piping for the bleed-air system can be seen when the Buccaneer's wings are folded

## "AT ITS HIGH POINT, MORE THAN 100 BUCCANEERS SERVED IN THE ROYAL AIR FORCE"

Huge clamshell-type air brakes gave the Buccaneer slow-speed agility

# DESIGN

The requirement was for a fast, jet-powered attack aircraft capable of flying slow enough to land on an aircraft carrier but also fast enough and with enough payload to fight against Soviet military shipping. This was a difficult task, as in 1952, jet technology was in its infancy.

Blackburn Aircraft won the contract with the Buccaneer S1, introduced in 1963. Its design had folding wings for storage on board, an arrestor hook for landings, plus a huge tail-mounted air brake to aid handling at low speeds. In addition, the Buccaneer employed an aerodynamic

technique known as 'flap blowing'. Bleed air was taken from the jet engines and blown over areas of the wings and flight-control surfaces to improve lift and enable the aircraft to respond better at low speeds. The piping for the bleed-air system can be seen inside of the wing structure when the aircraft has the wings folded. At the time, this technique, which is called Boundary Layer, was at the cutting edge of aerodynamics.

The initial S1 was underpowered, and while the aircraft had a good payload, an engine failure while at low speed landing or taking

off from a carrier was disastrous. To solve the issue, the S2 was developed with more powerful Rolls-Royce Spey engines. This aircraft had 40 per cent more power and significantly better fuel economy and went on to be highly successful until retirement in 1994.

The Buccaneer also featured an all-weather capability, something that was rare at the time. Early generation electronic flight systems controls, coupled with nose-mounted on-board radar, gave the aircraft the capability to fly at very low levels and high speeds in bad weather.

## POWERPLANT

The S1 Buccaneer was powered by the early generation De Havilland Gyron turbojet engine, delivering 7,100 pounds of thrust. With this power, the aircraft could not lift a full fuel tank as well as a full weapon load. In order to operate from aircraft carriers, the S1 had to take off with minimum fuel and then rendezvous with an in-flight refuelling aircraft to take on full fuel. Clearly, this was an inefficient fuelling system that had to be rectified.

The S2 was a modified Buccaneer with the Rolls-Royce Spey engine, significantly more powerful and giving the aircraft far greater versatility. The new engines required some modifications to the aircraft structure including the air intakes, but then proved to be highly successful.

"SPECIAL ROTATING BOMB BAY DOORS WERE DESIGNED TO OPEN UP TO THE MAXIMUM SPEED OF THE AIRCRAFT AT 0.9 MACH"

*The back-seat crewman was responsible for weapons systems and navigation and had a separate windscreen in the event of canopy jettison*

## ARMAMENT

Originally designed to deliver a nuclear weapon at Soviet warships, the diversity of the Buccaneer payloads over the years is symptomatic of the political attitude towards military spending of the time. The original weapon in the design was to be the 'Green Cheese' air-launched nuclear missile.

However, the development programme for the missile was cancelled, meaning that the Buccaneer first flew with the unguided 20-kiloton Red Beard bomb.

The aircraft had a fully concealed bomb bay to give it a high cruise speed at low level. This meant that special rotating bomb bay doors were designed to open up to the maximum speed of the aircraft at 0.9 mach.

The large weapons bay could also carry a range of other payloads, including conventional non-nuclear bombs. At the time it joined the Royal Navy, it could carry any payload that the navy had available. Early in its career, the Buccaneer carried conventional bombs against shipping, but

this was considered hazardous, as the low-level capability had to be sacrificed to climb and deliver the bombs. Eventually, the aircraft were upgraded to carry the stand-off capability Sea Eagle missile.

Buccaneers could also carry a photo-reconnaissance pod, plus a large ferry tank for positioning flights across the globe. Under-wing hardpoints could carry weapons. Laser designator systems extended the life of the aircraft, which often flew alongside the newer Tornado in support.

*The original Buccaneer was designed for nuclear weapons delivery*

*A test shot of a Red Beard bomb, the first British tactical nuclear weapon*

*Both crew members sat on early generation Martin Baker ejection seats. Early jet era instrumentation could be haphazard in layout*

# COCKPIT

The crew of two flew in a tandem cockpit configuration, seated in early generation Martin Baker ejection seats. The combination of early generation electronic weapons technology and mechanical flight instruments made the cockpit layout a little haphazard at first glance. No modern heads-up displays were available at this time, meaning the pilot had to look inside for all instrument displays.

The rear-seat crew member operated the weapons and, later, electronic countermeasures, plus the nose-mounted radar and weapons-control systems. A large single-piece canopy covered the crew. This could be jettisoned in the event of ejection, with the rear-seat crewman having an additional windscreen for protection against the high-speed air blast.

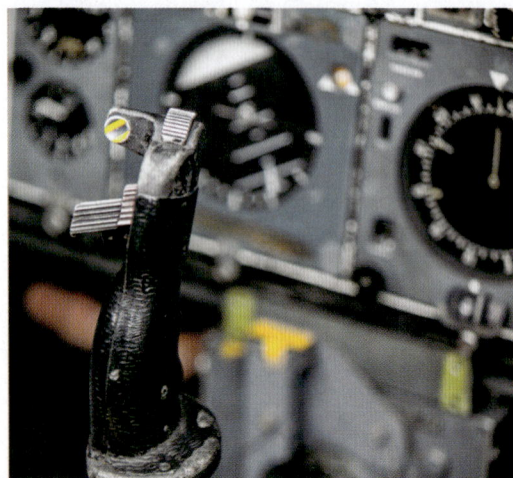

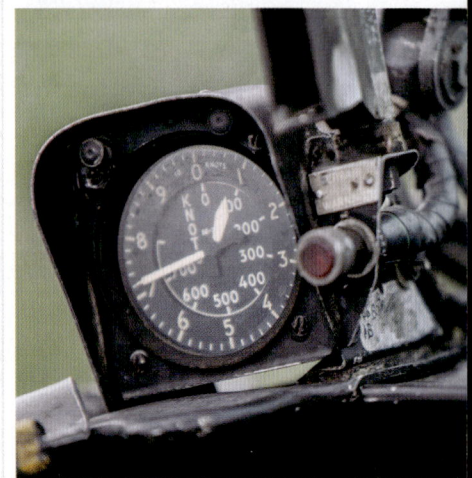

*In the first Gulf War, Buccaneers were repainted and re-equipped in just 72 hours for a desert warfare role*

# ROLES AND DIVERSITY

While the Buccaneer was effective in its original role as a fast maritime strike aircraft, it is perhaps best known as a Royal Air Force jet. Blackburn originally proposed the aircraft to the RAF as a replacement to the Canberra. The Royal Air Force insisted that their new jet had to be supersonic, so the Buccaneer was discounted. However, at this time, in the mid 1960s, there was much political upheaval in the procurement of military equipment, with spending cuts, inter-force distrust and rivalry as the British Army, Navy and Air Force each fought to defend their budgets and capability.

With the controversial cancellation of the TSR2 project, the Blackburn offer was revisited. Additionally, the controversial 1957 White Paper on defence spending called for the retirement of Navy aircraft carriers, with the Royal Air Force tasked with assuming the capability of striking against maritime targets. While the RAF may have been reluctant to take the Buccaneer, it proved to be a very useful asset. As the

Panavia Tornado programme was delayed, it continued to serve a useful role. Even after the introduction of the Tornado, it continued to fly missions. Probably the most famous was the rapid deployment at short notice in the 1991 Gulf War. Re-equipped and repainted in desert camouflage in less than 72 hours, the Buccaneers flew with laser designation guidance systems. Flying alongside two Tornados, the Buccaneer used the laser to 'designate' the target for the smart bomb that was then delivered by the Tornado. This teamwork delivered a huge amount of damage to bridges and other infrastructure. Additionally, Buccaneers delivered their own weapons, one such mission managing to hit two Iraqi aircraft while still taxiing on the ground.

Despite the introduction of more modern aircraft alongside it, including the Harrier and the Jaguar, the Buccaneer continued to play a very cost-effective and useful role amid the constantly changing political backdrop of the 1957 White Paper, the end of the Cold War and the subsequent 1991 Gulf War.

*Below, left to right:*
*The pilot's joystick operated hydraulically boosted flying surfaces*

*Early jet cockpits had no heads-up display. The second airspeed indicator aided carrier landings*

*Cold War jet cockpits were designed for functionality above all else*

# TECH STATS

The particular aircraft in these photographs is XN974, the very first production S2 Buccaneer. This aircraft was sent to the Royal Aeronautical Establishment for trials and testing and then on to HMS Eagle for sea trials. It then flew to the USA, where it was used in Nevada for hot-weather testing.

XN974 was used continually throughout its life as a development test bed. As the political and military climate changed, weapons systems were introduced and new electric warfare systems designed, this aircraft was used for testing the systems before they went live with frontline squadrons. It is preserved in ground running condition at Yorkshire Air Museum, where it is often seen taxiing on the runways at events.

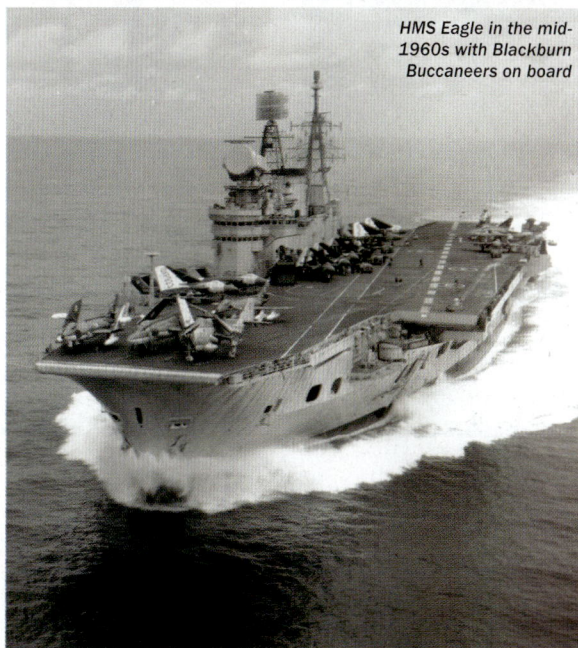

*HMS Eagle in the mid-1960s with Blackburn Buccaneers on board*

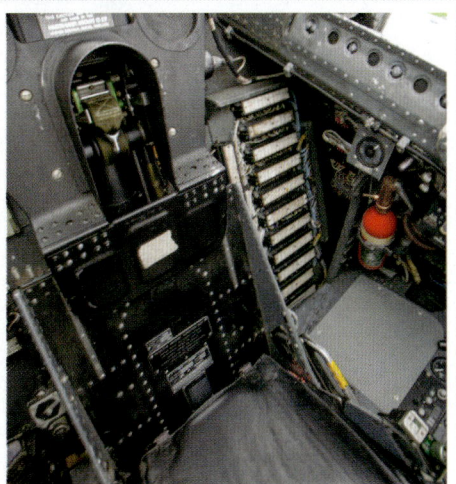

Operation Desert Storm hit Iraq like a force of nature and heralded its decline from a regional power to a failed state, yet the story from inside Saddam's regime is rarely told...

# IN THE EYE OF DESERT STORM

WORDS: TALLHA ABDULRAZAQ

As has been the case since time immemorial, history is almost always written by the victors. The United States of America's rise to global power and dominance is a popular story, one told countless times over. However, what's rarely seen is an Iraqi perspective of the Gulf War.

While most observers focus on Saddam's expansionist agenda, they tend to neglect the Iraqi military, which is often a silent witness, barely considered in most histories of the war. Since the collapse of Saddam's Ba'athist regime after the US-led invasion in 2003, the archives of Saddam's secretive government have been laid bare for historians to pore over. It is now time for this iconic war to be revisited, and for the record to be re-examined. After all, this war was so devastating to the Iraqi military and state, it became etched into the Iraqi conscience as 'The Mother of Battles'.

After the Iran-Iraq War between 1980 and 1988, the Iraqi military was regionally viewed in much the same light as the Prussian military was among the Europeans after Moltke the Elder's successful campaigns in 1866-71. The Iraqi Army had developed a reputation for endurance, steadfastness and professionalism after its operations with Iran towards the end of the war that allowed Iraq to emerge victorious, if only just. At least compared to other Arab armies, who suffered a slew of defeats at the hands of Israel, the Iraqi Army came to be feared and respected.

This reputation was soon to be tested, this time against the military might of the Western world led by the only global superpower – the United States of America.

## Kuwait – Iraq's 19th province

Since Iraq gained at least nominal independence from British colonial rule, it had made territorial claims over the country of Kuwait, believing it to be an integral part of its southern Basra region. After a bloody struggle with the Ayatollahs, Saddam's coffers were empty and the state was saddled with immense debts of $30 billion to neighbouring Arab Gulf countries alone. With a tanking economy and decreasing oil revenue, resulting from an increase in his Arab neighbours' oil production that deflated prices, Saddam was under increasing pressure to act. When he failed to get his Arab creditors to relieve Iraq's debt burden through diplomacy, and with increasing whispers in Baghdad of a potential military coup against him, Saddam needed a show of strength and a distraction for his army all at once. He needed another war.

Saddam felt like he had been betrayed by his Arab brothers. In his eyes, Iraqi blood had been spilt for eight years in order to stop the fundamentalist Islamic Revolution of Ayatollah Khomeini from expanding into the rest of the Arab world. Rather than acknowledging Iraq's sacrifice, Saddam and his aides believed that their Arab neighbours were trying to weaken Iraq by keeping it indebted and with a weak economy. As Iraq's smallest neighbour, and as it shared the enormous Rumaila oil field, Kuwait was the obvious target for Iraqi ire, and would serve as a suitable demonstration of force that would browbeat the other Arabs into acquiescence. Iraq began to mobilise on 15 July 1990 and deployed troops on the Iraqi-Kuwaiti border as a last-ditch effort to intimidate the Kuwaitis into capitulating. When this failed, the invasion of Kuwait was ordered, and plans were drawn up.

Not much time was allotted for the Iraqi officers to plan their invasion. Primary responsibility for the invasion of Kuwait lay with the Republican Guard, commanded by Lieutenant General Ayad Futayyih al-Rawi. His operational plan was as follows:

The Republican Guard's 3rd Special Forces Brigade were to make an airborne landing in Kuwait City, the Kuwaiti capital, to capture the Emir of Kuwait's palace and other government buildings. They would be supported by forces from the Hammurabi Armoured Division, who would be thrusting down the main road connecting Iraq and Kuwait. Meanwhile, forces from the Nebuchadnezzar Infantry Division were tasked with establishing control over Kuwait City once the Special Forces Brigade had established control over primary targets.

A further Republican Guard infantry brigade was to penetrate Kuwait from the Iraqi town of Umm Qasr and move to gain control over the Kuwaiti island of Bubiyan, thus establishing Iraqi control north of Kuwait City.

The Republican Guard Medina Armoured Division was to drive on Ahmadi to secure the south of Kuwait City and cut it off from the south of Kuwait. This movement was to be supported by the Adnan Infantry Division, which would secure Kuwait's southern borders with Saudi Arabia. After the war with Iran, Iraq had a fleet of 750 combat aircraft, which,

*Soldiers of the Iraqi Army line up during the Iran-Iraq war of 1980-88*

*Sipa Press/REX*

# SADDAM'S REPUBLICAN GUARD

**THE IRAQI REPUBLICAN GUARD WAS THE CREAM OF THE IRAQI MILITARY CROP, USED TO DETER ENEMIES BOTH AT HOME AND ABROAD**

The Republican Guard was the best of Iraq's ground forces. Originally formed in 1969 as a single brigade based in Baghdad, the Republican Guard's main role before the Iran-Iraq War was to prevent the Regular Army from making any coup attempts or overthrowing the government. Modern Iraqi history is replete with examples of bloody

*Iraqi officers plan their next moves as Operation Desert Storm closes in on them*

putsches bringing new leaders and ideologies to power, and so the Republican Guard was formed as a Praetorian force to act as a deterrent against military officers who had ambitions above their station.
During the desperation of the Iran-Iraq War, the Republican Guard was expanded into eight divisions, given the

## NUMBERS
Eight divisions, approx 200,000 men – two armoured, one mechanised, four infantry and one special forces.

## ARMOUR
Made use of BMP Armoured Personnel Carriers, T-72 Main Battle Tanks (including some Lions of Babylon, a T-72 variant), and 155mm self-propelled howitzers.

## WEAPONS
Infantry weapons include AK-47, RPK Light Machine Guns, PKT General-Purpose Machine Guns, Makarov pistols and RPG-7.

best military equipment that Iraq could afford and granted privileges beyond other units. This made them into Iraq's premier fighting force, answerable only to Saddam himself. The best recruits and officers were given over to the Republican Guard. They were used as a strategic reserve to shore up weaker Iraqi units as well as an offensive force deployed to deal with the hardest operational challenges the Iraqi military had to face. They were responsible for retaking the Faw Peninsula from occupying Iranian forces near the end of the Iran-Iraq War, as well as contributing decisively to operations that led to the defeat and withdrawal of the Iranian military, which subsequently ended the war. Due to their proficiency and effectiveness, Saddam came to rely upon them more and more throughout his military adventures, and used them to spearhead the invasion of Kuwait in 1990.

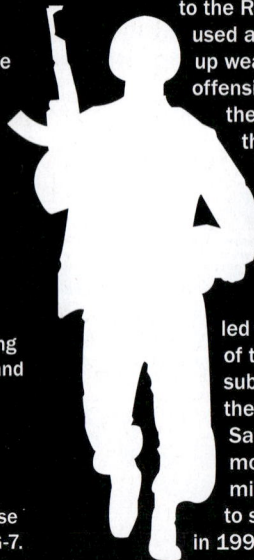

in conjunction with the relatively small land mass of Kuwait placing airfields within easy range of Iraqi ground forces, gave them a high expectation of achieving and maintaining complete control of the skies. Such was their confidence that orders were issued to Iraqi commanders specifically instructing them to avoid destroying the Kuwaiti air force and navy, presumably so that Iraq could seize this equipment for itself.

The Kuwaiti Army was held in similarly low esteem, as a total of six brigades (one mechanised, two armoured, two commando, and a single Royal Guard brigade) were all the forces that Kuwait had to defend an area of less than 7,000 square miles against a vastly superior Iraqi force of 100,000. The Iraqis were both qualitatively and quantitatively superior to the Kuwaitis, outnumbering them by an enormous nine to one.

The invasion began in the early hours of 2 August 1990 in a two-pronged attack. Iraqi Special Forces were deployed via helicopter in Kuwait City as planned, while the Hammurabi Division drove south down Route 80 (soon to become infamous as the 'Highway of Death') directly towards Kuwait City. The Medina Armoured Division's thrust came down a road slightly farther to the west, before making a hook to the east to take up the positions outlined in the Iraqi campaign plan. It was at this moment that one of the rare few clashes with Kuwaiti forces began, but it proved to be a lacklustre affair.

At approximately 6.45am, the Kuwaiti 35th Armoured Brigade quite literally ran afoul of elements of the Iraqi 17th Armoured Brigade, commanded by then Brigadier General Ra'ad al-Hamdani. After their British-made Chieftain tanks received a volley of Iraqi T-72 fire into their flanks, the Kuwaiti brigade melted away, returning inaccurate fire that managed to take out just one Iraqi tank in this initial action.

In personal memoirs detailing his part in the conquest of Kuwait, al-Hamdani reported that the Iraqi forces were ordered to use non-lethal rounds when firing upon Kuwaiti armour in order to minimise casualties and to scare the defending forces into surrender rather than be forced to utterly destroy them. Al-Hamdani suggests that this is because many military commanders still saw the Kuwaitis as their Arab brothers, and, considering the overwhelming number of Iraqis, saw no need to deploy disproportionate force for what was a foregone conclusion of a total Iraqi victory.

This conclusion came to pass less than 12 hours after the operation started. Apart from a small engagement with a brigade

> "THE IRAQIS WERE BOTH QUALITATIVELY AND QUANTITATIVELY SUPERIOR TO THE KUWAITIS, OUTNUMBERING THEM BY AN ENORMOUS NINE TO ONE"

# THE ORIGINAL COALITION OF THE WILLING
### THE USA WASN'T ALONE IN ITS OPERATION AGAINST IRAQ'S OCCUPATION

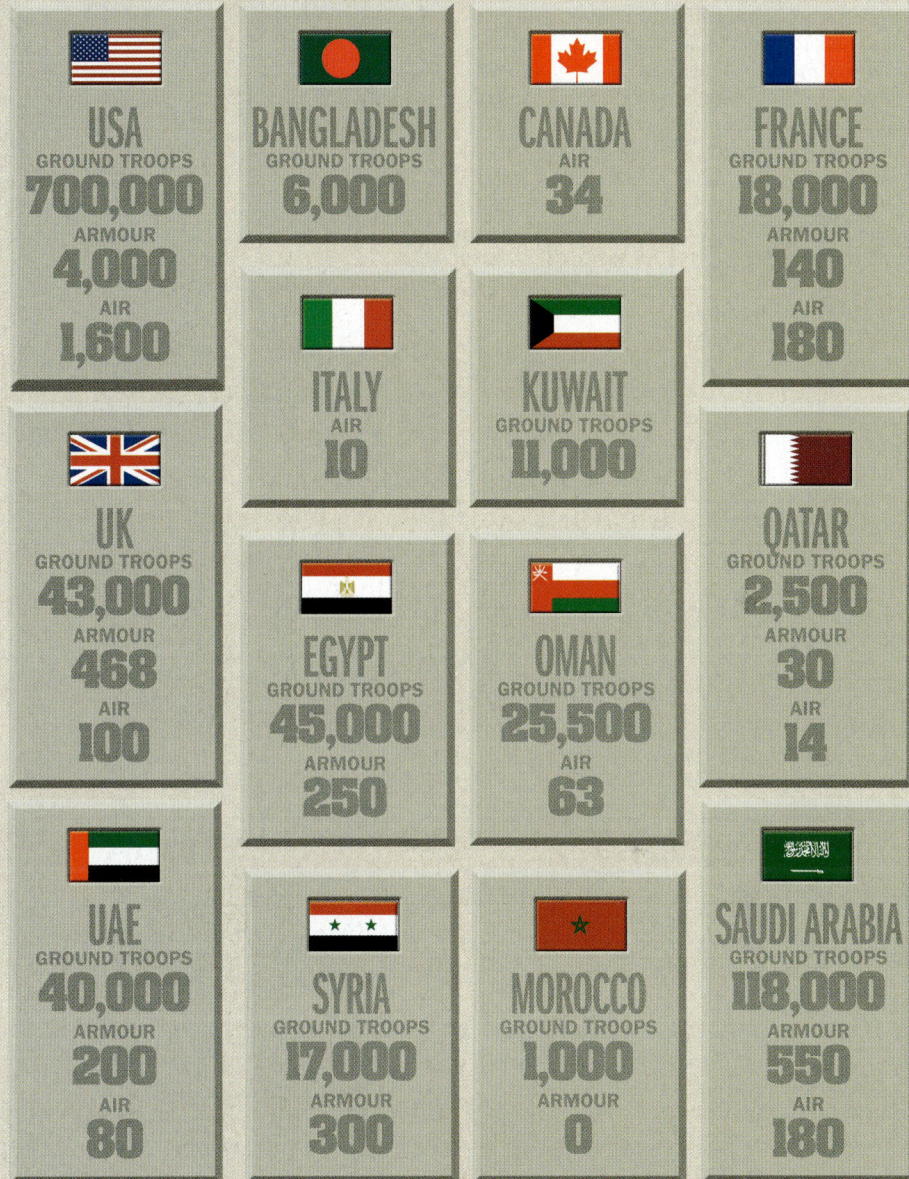

**USA**
GROUND TROOPS
700,000
ARMOUR
4,000
AIR
1,600

**BANGLADESH**
GROUND TROOPS
6,000

**CANADA**
AIR
34

**FRANCE**
GROUND TROOPS
18,000
ARMOUR
140
AIR
180

**ITALY**
AIR
10

**KUWAIT**
GROUND TROOPS
11,000

**UK**
GROUND TROOPS
43,000
ARMOUR
468
AIR
100

**EGYPT**
GROUND TROOPS
45,000
ARMOUR
250

**OMAN**
GROUND TROOPS
25,500
AIR
63

**QATAR**
GROUND TROOPS
2,500
ARMOUR
30
AIR
14

**UAE**
GROUND TROOPS
40,000
ARMOUR
200
AIR
80

**SYRIA**
GROUND TROOPS
17,000
ARMOUR
300

**MOROCCO**
GROUND TROOPS
1,000
ARMOUR
0

**SAUDI ARABIA**
GROUND TROOPS
118,000
ARMOUR
550
AIR
180

## VS

# THE IRAQI ARMY

THE IRAQI ARMY FACED THE IMPOSSIBLE TASK OF FIGHTING AGAINST A COALITION OF 1,000,000 MEN, WITH ARMOUR AND COMBAT AIRCRAFT NUMBERING IN THE THOUSANDS USING ONLY THE FOLLOWING:

| ARMOUR | GROUND TROOPS | AIR |
| --- | --- | --- |
| 4,200 | 600,000 | 750 |

of Kuwaiti Royal Guardsmen at the Emir of Kuwait's palace that led to the death of Fahad Al Sabah, the emir's younger brother, Iraq was in near total control. Over the next few days, Iraqi forces consolidated their control over Kuwait and mopped up any remaining pockets of resistance before Saddam formally announced that Kuwait had "joined" Iraq as its 19th province. The Kuwaiti royal family had fled almost as soon as Iraqi forces had crossed the border, their military units were either captured or had also fled to Saudi Arabia, and Kuwait no longer existed as a sovereign state.

Although the Iraqi forces had easily conquered Kuwait, it's highly likely they might not have celebrated their victory so eagerly had they known what kind of storm was brewing on the horizon.

## The gathering storm

Immediately after Iraq invaded Kuwait, the international community, led by the United States, condemned the invasion and a series of United Nations Security Council resolutions were passed, demanding a complete Iraqi withdrawal and placing Iraq under sanctions.

Perhaps attempting to see if he could make the world blink first, Saddam refused to withdraw Iraqi forces from Kuwait, leading to a Western and allied Arab military buildup in the region. Strategically, the United States feared what would happen if Iraq launched an invasion of oil-rich Saudi Arabia, thus placing most of the world's oil supply directly under Saddam's control, or at the very least threatened by him. However, this was not in Saddam's mind at all. Iraqi sources show that, at a very basic level, all Saddam wanted was to restore the Iraqi economy and he hoped to use Kuwait as a bargaining chip to obtain concessions

*With the Iraqi air force destroyed in the early stages of the war, unstoppable strikes from the air halted ground troops*

# THE LION OF BABYLON TANK

THE 'LION OF BABYLON' WAS AN IRAQI-MODIFIED SOVIET T-72 TANK THAT SOUNDED MORE FEARSOME THAN IT PROVED ON THE FIELD OF BATTLE

### EFFECTIVE COMBAT RANGE
The effective combat engagement range of this tank was 1.8km, which was meagre compared to the British Challenger or the American M1 Abrams tanks.

### ENGINE
With a V-12 diesel engine producing an underwhelming 780bhp, the Lion was capable of average speeds of 45km/h with an operational range of a maximum of 600km.

### MAIN ARMAMENT
The tank's main punch came from its 125mm main gun, which could fire armour-piercing sabot rounds, HEAT and HEF ammunition.

### SECONDARY ARMAMENTS
The Iraqis tended to use tanks as self-propelled artillery or in support of infantry operations, and so a 7.62mm PKT coaxial machine gun was the secondary weapon of choice.

### ARMOUR
While its armour was primarily steel plate ranging between 45-300mm, one Iraqi innovation was to use additional 30mm 'spaced armour' frontal laminate plates to dissipate the effects of HEAT rounds.

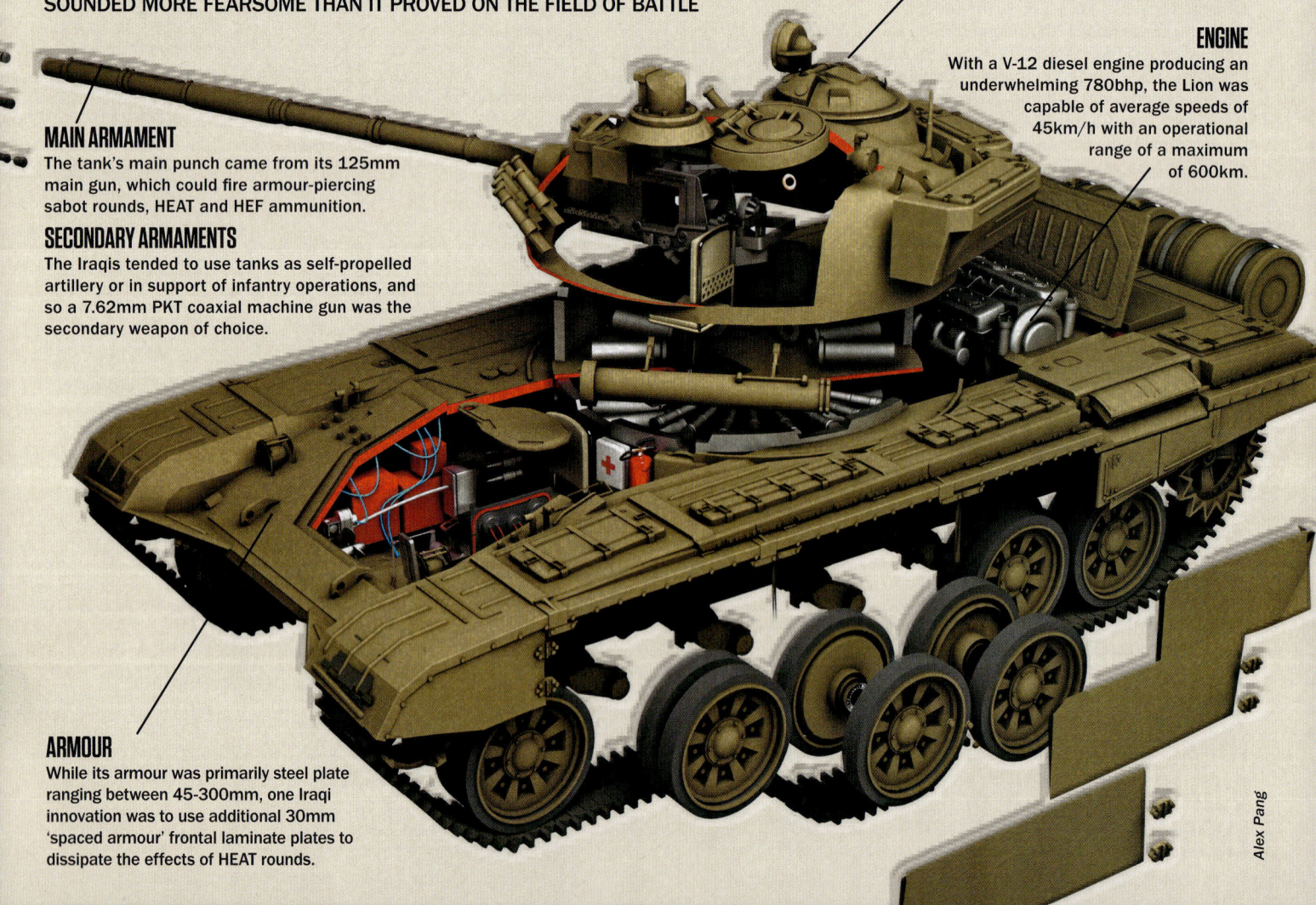

Alex Pang

from his neighbours and the international community. This certainly explains why the Iraqi Army sat still and watched as an international force nearing 1,000,000 soldiers and support personnel slowly amassed over a period of almost six months as a part of what was named Operation Desert Shield.

The Iraqi Army was forbidden from pre-emptively striking at the build up of the American-led Coalition Forces, and was instead left to ponder how best to weather the storm about to break over their heads. In an excellent example of how questioning Saddam's world view was detrimental to a man's military career, the Iraqi Army Chief of Staff, General Nizar al-Khazraji, was forced into retirement for suggesting that Iraqi forces should withdraw back to Iraq and end hostilities. The rest of the Iraqi staff officers knew that Saddam could easily take more than their jobs and already had a well-established reputation of having officers who displeased him killed. They soon presented Saddam with a defensive plan that made his strategic requirement of holding Kuwait their priority, even though they were very aware that this was a losing gambit, effectively paralysing the Iraqi military before combat operations had even begun.

Iraqi planners understood very well that the primary objective of the Coalition would be to destroy as much of Iraq's air power infrastructure as possible, including attacks on aircraft and airfields. Nonetheless, and contrary to their experiences of the Iraqi air force's dire performance during the Iran-Iraq War, they planned to use air power to provide support to Iraqi ground forces.

The Iraqi Army was to mobilise all its reserves and prepare to deploy the majority of an army of 600,000 men into prepared, dug-in defensive positions. The Republican Guard would be used as a strategic reserve only upon the order of Saddam himself, and they were positioned just north of the Kuwaiti border with the intention that they would shore up any of the weaker Iraqi Army units.

The Iraqi plan was essentially to fight a conventional war against the best-equipped, trained and supplied conventional military force in the world. Saddam's obsession with holding captured territory and not relinquishing it to better serve military aims stems from the way he conducted the Iraqi invasion of Iran. Rather than give up territory that was not essential to military objectives, Saddam made his soldiers fight tooth and nail for seemingly little gain. A mere few years after the Iran-Iraq War ended, and history was already repeating itself.

In a desperate attempt to even the odds, al-Hamdani claims that the Iraqi Command even authorised the use of Scud missiles as well as kamikaze pilots against coalition naval units, such as aircraft carriers. Scud missiles are notoriously inaccurate, as Iraqi attempts were to shortly prove, and even thinking of depending on suicidal pilots demonstrates the desperate situation Iraqi commanders were in.

## The storm breaks

Not long after Saddam failed to heed the 15 January 1991 deadline for Iraq to withdraw, Operation Desert Storm was unleashed upon Iraqi forces at 2.30 am on 17 January. For

## "SADDAM REFUSED TO WITHDRAW IRAQI FORCES FROM KUWAIT, LEADING TO A WESTERN AND ALLIED ARAB MILITARY BUILDUP IN THE REGION"

39 days, the Coalition conducted an intense strategic bombing campaign that hammered Iraqi military and civilian infrastructure, notoriously killing 408 civilians who were taking shelter in Baghdad's Amiriyah bomb shelter.

Iraqi aircraft, air defences, early warning radar systems and Army Air Aviation units were destroyed in order to achieve complete command of the skies. The Coalition's complete dominance over the airspace made Iraqi command and control facilities easy targets and were subsequently obliterated, further crippling Iraq's ability to mount a successful defence. Next on the hit list was

the Iraqi military itself, although many Iraqi defensive positions, honed after eight years of war with Iran, proved to be successful at preserving most of the units sheltering there. All in all, more than 100,000 sorties were flown against Iraqi targets, dropping a devastating 88,500 tons of bombs.

Never wanting it to be said that the Iraqi military took a severe bombing lying down, the first real ground engagement of Desert Storm took place on 29 January – after Iraqi forces attempted an offensive to throw the coalition off balance and bring the war back down to the ground, where they hoped to fare better.

The Iraqi 5th Mechanised Division, alongside a supporting brigade from both the 3rd Armoured Division and the 1st Mechanised Division, thrust over the Kuwaiti-Saudi border to take the Saudi port town of Khafji ten kilometres away. Moments after Iraqi forces began to move, they were repeatedly hammered by Coalition airstrikes. Nonetheless, the Iraqis still managed to take Khafji.

This victory was very short-lived, however, as throughout the next two days Iraqi forces

*Iraqi soldiers, pictured in 1990, raise their AK-47s in a show of support for their country*

Sipa Press/REX

# THE HIGHWAY OF DEATH

**AS IRAQI FORCES FLED KUWAIT, COALITION AIRCRAFT LED BY THE UNITED STATES DEVASTATED THEM, LEAVING BURNING WRECKAGES ON HIGHWAY 80**

On the night of 26 February 1991, Iraqi forces ceased combat operations in Kuwait and began withdrawing along the main highway back to Iraq. This large movement of troops and vehicles formed an enormous convoy of closely packed military targets that coalition aircraft, spearheaded by the US Air Force, took as an opportunity to deal a devastating blow. The withdrawing convoy was subjected to such intense aerial bombardment that by the next day the entire highway was littered with smouldering corpses and burning tank hulks. The Iraqi forces stood no chance, as the coalition had already previously neutralised the Iraqi air force and air defence systems, and gained complete air superiority.

This stretch of highway gained the moniker of 'the Highway of Death' due to almost 2,000 Iraqi vehicles being destroyed and possibly thousands of Iraqi men found killed either still in their vehicles or on the side of the road after trying to escape. To this day, there is no accurate account of exactly how many Iraqi soldiers lost their lives on the Highway of Death, but it is clear that after this event the Iraqi military would never be the same again.

*A small stretch of road on the Highway of Death. Even civilian vehicles were caught in the carnage*

*The twisted metal and wrecked hull of an Iraqi tank. The tank crew would not have survived*

## "TO THIS DAY, THERE IS NO ACCURATE ACCOUNT OF EXACTLY HOW MANY IRAQI SOLDIERS LOST THEIR LIVES ON THE HIGHWAY OF DEATH"

*An American soldier inspects the carbonised bodies of Iraqi soldiers who were killed when their convoy of vehicles was bombed as they attempted to retreat from Kuwait*

in Khafji were besieged in the town they had just taken. Coming under heavy bombardment from American airstrikes while also fending off attacks from elements of the US 3rd Marine Regiment and the Saudi 2nd National Guard Brigade, the Iraqis were unable to reinforce their positions due to Coalition air interdiction missions preventing any further significant Iraqi penetrations into Saudi territory. After resisting for two days, the Iraqis were forced to surrender and Khafji was recaptured on 1 February, with Iraqi casualties numbering 554 men.

Coalition airstrikes showed no signs of letting up, and apart from the Battle of Khafji, the Iraqis made no further attempts to force the coalition into a ground war. This was not because they had given up, but simply because they were denied any opportunity. Instead, they maintained their defensive positions until Coalition forces finally gave the Iraqis the land offensive they had desired for more than a month. 24 February 1991 will long be a date remembered as when the Iraqi military jumped out of the frying pan and into the fire. Over the next 100 hours, the war would be decided in favour of the coalition, with Iraq's military forces severely damaged.

Under the overall command of US General Norman Schwarzkopf, Coalition ground units launched a spearhead into Kuwait from the south after creating feints to make the Iraqis believe the coalition would invade across Iraq's southern border with Saudi Arabia. Most Iraqi units were incredibly hungry after months of sanctions, and officers reported having to eat bread that was as hard as stone to survive. This had a devastating affect on troop morale, with soldiers surrendering en masse to attacking Coalition forces.

Iraq's border with Saudi Arabia is about 810 kilometres long, and with most of the Iraqi forces focused in static defensive positions in the south east of Iraq and inside Kuwait itself, this left the Iraqis vulnerable to being flanked. The US 7th Corps attacked from the south and fixed the Iraqi forces, and the US 18th Airborne Corps executed a large sweep farther to the west, driving into the Iraqi desert before turning east to cut off Iraqi units attempting to escape. However, the main threat to American plans was still the Republican Guard.

As Saddam's strategic reserve, and having just sustained more than a month of airstrikes, the Republican Guard put up a valiant attempt at salvaging an impossible situation. On the last full day of fighting in Desert Storm, the Republican Guard at least were capable of being the only unit to temporarily force an American withdrawal.

The Medina Division's 2nd Brigade had entrenched its tanks in defilade along a ridge about 36 kilometres from the Kuwaiti border to conceal their presence from the advancing US 1st Armored Division. With no air support, the Republican Guardsmen attacked ferociously, their anti-aircraft batteries able to shoot down one American A-10 bomber, which forced the American commander to temporarily withdraw his forces to a safer distance, before recommencing attack and eventually overcoming this Republican Guard force.

Realising the futility of continuing the war, and as he watched his forces melting away around him, Saddam called for a full withdrawal from Kuwait on 27 February. Retreating Iraqi forces fled back up Route 80, but were bombed relentlessly, creating the carnage we now know as the Highway of Death.

By the time US President George HW Bush declared a ceasefire on 28 February, Iraqi casualties amounted to more than 200,000, including 35,000 fatalities and 63,000 soldiers captured. In comparison, the Coalition's KIA list of 341 was very light indeed. After facing down an alliance of 34 countries, hundreds of thousands of soldiers and thousands of tanks and aircraft, Iraq had lost the Gulf War. The results of Iraq's military misadventure in the Gulf cost it not only a large part of its forces, but also led to it being placed under a merciless sanctions regime that crippled the Iraqi economy and led to the deaths of hundreds of thousands of civilians.

Operation Desert Storm was named 'The Mother of Battles' because, in all its history since its foundation in 1921, the Iraqi Armed Forces had never faced such a devastating campaign of annihilation. The losses suffered by Iraq in one of the most ferocious military campaigns in history presaged the beginning of many long years of suffering that continues to this day.

# THE DANGER OF QUESTIONING ORDERS

**LIEUTENANT GENERAL RA'AD AL-HAMDANI, A FORMER COMMANDER IN THE IRAQI REPUBLICAN GUARD, WROTE ABOUT HIS GULF WAR EXPERIENCES AND THE DANGERS OF QUESTIONING SUPERIOR OFFICERS**

"I had the audacity to criticise the Iraqi war plan… The primary problem with [the plan] was that it was based upon the experience of the Iran-Iraq War and was designed taking these precedents into account. The plan should have taken into account the new military environment where we would be facing armies that are at the peak of any standard witnessed throughout military history.

"This military environment was completely different from the one we knew during our war with Iran… and we would be unable to execute our plans due to the overwhelming air superiority enjoyed by the enemy that would make its presence known within days of combat commencing. This air superiority would restrict our movements while granting the enemy full operational freedom of movement in comparison to us.

"As was customary in the Iraqi military, my criticisms were considered unacceptable and politically unjustifiable. My critique was mocked, and one senior officer stated: 'These words are dangerous and clearly run contrary to the wishes and guidance of the President [Saddam Hussein]. They are an attempt to diminish our morale, and your suggestions serve the interests of the enemy.'

"A military investigation committee was set up immediately to investigate what I meant by my words, and if I was truly doubting the orders of the President… I later found out that the man who saved me from these accusations was none other than Qusay, the son of President Saddam Hussein, who had served with me on the front in the Iran-Iraq War in 1983."

## "WE WOULD BE UNABLE TO EXECUTE OUR PLANS DUE TO THE OVERWHELMING AIR SUPERIORITY ENJOYED BY THE ENEMY"

*Iraqi soldiers in Kuwait wave white flags as they surrender to the Coalition forces*

*US aircraft taking off to take part in Operation Desert Storm*

أم المعارك

## "THE MOTHER OF BATTLES"

THE IRAQI NAME FOR THE 1990 GULF WAR

*An Iraqi prisoner of war is searched at gunpoint after being captured by US Marines*

"24 FEBRUARY 1991 WILL LONG BE A DATE REMEMBERED AS WHEN THE IRAQI MILITARY JUMPED OUT OF THE FRYING PAN AND INTO THE FIRE. OVER THE NEXT 100 HOURS, THE WAR WOULD BE DECIDED IN FAVOUR OF THE COALITION, WITH IRAQ'S MILITARY FORCES SEVERELY DAMAGED"

# THE LIBERATION OF KUWAIT

## In around 100 hours the Coalition ground offensive defeated Iraq's occupation forces and liberated the capital city

*Kuwaiti civilians celebrate in the streets after the arrival of Coalition forces*

**WORDS:** TIM WILLIAMSON

Early in the morning of 24 February, the Coalition finally launched the ground offensive of Operation Desert Storm, called Desert Sabre. Despite 40 days of aerial bombardment targeting Iraqi defences, logistics, as well as command and control targets, dislodging Saddam's occupation forces was expected to be a costly challenge for the outnumbered coalition troops. Expecting the attack, the Iraqis had focused on fortifying the southern border, laying minefields, and building up defensive banks to block enemy vehicles.

While General Schwarzkopf's divisions launched their surprise left hook, penetrating deep into Iraq from the north-west before later turning east to cut off the Iraqis, Coalition forces positioned along the Saudi-Kuwaiti border pushed directly north and north-east towards the capital. These included divisions from the Coalition's Arab nations, under the command of Lt. Gen. Khaled bin Sultan, flanking American divisions who would make the main thrust north to Kuwait City.

Despite being slowed slightly by the Iraqi defences, US Marines were able to smash or literally bulldoze their way north – their tanks fitted with bulldozer blades and forked mine ploughs that made short work of the sand banks and minefields. The sheer firepower of the US artillery and armour overwhelmed Saddam's regular forces, who were outmatched at every level, especially in their ageing and vulnerable T-55 tanks. At the end of the first day the US Marines progressed 20 miles inside Kuwait, capturing 10,000 Iraqi POWs. On 25 February, coincidentally the same date Kuwait marked the 30th anniversary of its independence, Saddam ordered his occupation forces to withdraw. The advance into Kuwait continued, and the following day American forces surrounded the capital. Meanwhile, Kuwaiti resistance forces inside Kuwait City declared they had gained control. On 26-27 February, Lt. Gen. Khaled's divisions moved past their American allies to lead the liberation of the city. Having the city freed by fellow Arab forces, as well as the Kuwaitis themselves, was deemed politically and diplomatically appropriate. Despite the odds, a desperate final stand was mounted by the 3rd Iraqi Armoured Division at Kuwait International Airport, with the staggering loss of 100 tanks and thousands killed or captured.

Calling a ceasefire, President Bush demanded that Iraq comply with all the UN Security Council's resolutions, and return all hostages – to which Iraq agreed on 28 February, effectively ending the war. It took just 100 hours to drive the Iraqis out and liberate Kuwait, during which time over 60,000 of the occupiers surrendered to Coalition forces, and thousands lay dead in the desert sands.

## "HAVING THE CITY FREED BY FELLOW ARAB FORCES, AS WELL AS THE KUWAITIS THEMSELVES, WAS DEEMED POLITICALLY AND DIPLOMATICALLY APPROPRIATE"

Soldiers from the Kuwaiti army pray before continuing the attack towards the capital, 24 February, 1991

Images: Getty Images, Alamy

# GULF WAR SYNDROME

After the end of hostilities,
veterans began reporting a strange
combination of symptoms, the cause
of which remains a mystery

**WORDS: TIM WILLIAMSON**

After the end of the war, thousands of Coalition veterans reported a mystery illness. Symptoms include fatigue, muscle pain, rashes, diarrhoea and cognitive difficulties, as well as psychological conditions often associated with post-traumatic stress disorder.

Of the 700,000 US veterans who served in the war, the US government estimated that between 25-30% – between 175,000 and 210,000 – have suffered with the mystery illness, the cause of which there are several unconfirmed theories.

One of the main suspected causes of the syndrome is chemical or biological weapons. Prior to the outbreak of the war, it was feared that Saddam's forces would unleash their stockpile of chemical and biological weapons. During its war with Iran, Iraq had already resorted to using nerve agents such as sarin and tabun against the Iranians, killing tens of thousands. As well as gas masks and other protective equipment and drills, Nerve Agent Pre-treatment Sets (NAPS), and a number of other preventative measures were distributed to Coalition troops before the ground operation. Vaccination against anthrax poisoning and even plague – both feared to be potentially used by Iraq – was also carried out. Some of these medical countermeasures have

also been alleged to have caused Gulf War Syndrome. Even if the Iraqis did not choose to deploy their toxic weapons, there was also a high risk that they could be released as a result of Coalition air strikes, or other combat. After the ceasefire, in March, US forces conducting security operations in the city of Khamisiyah located and demolished what they thought was an ammunition storage and bunker complex – in fact the facility contained thousands of rockets filled with toxic sarin and cyclosarin. Approximately 100,000 service personnel were thought to have been exposed to these released nerve agents.

Tragically, exposure to toxins and harmful chemicals was not exclusively a result of enemy weapons. Another potential cause of the syndrome has been identified in the application of organophosphate pesticides on personnel. These were reportedly used to protect against fly-borne disease in the difficult desert conditions.

Later reports suggested these pesticides may have been sourced locally, without proper safety checks or precautions against extreme exposure to the chemical. Whatever the cause, the syndrome has affected thousands of veterans, decades after the end of the fighting, and the battle for fair compensation for veterans and their families continues to be waged to this day.

*British Gulf War veterans marking the 20th anniversary of the war's end, and campaigning for compensation for Gulf War Syndrome sufferers*

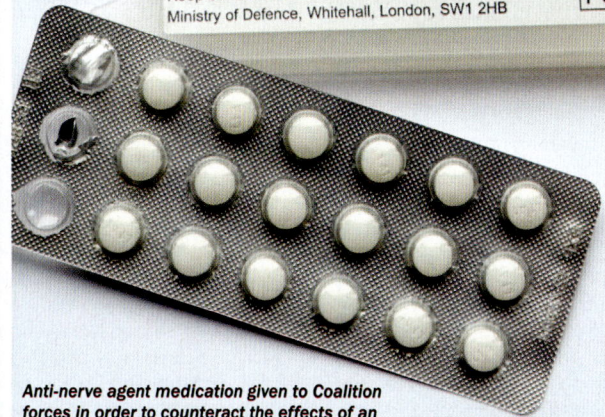

Nerve Agent Pre-Treatment Tablet Set L1A1 (NAPS L1A1)
Pyridostigmine Bromide
NATO Stock No: 6505-99-225-2344

1. Commence taking only when ordered by your commander.
2. Swallow one tablet by mouth every 8 hours.
3. Do not exceed the stated dose. Read leaflet for warnings.

31.5mg pyridostigmine bromide x 21 tablets
Keep out of the reach of children. Protect from moisture.
Ministry of Defence, Whitehall, London, SW1 2HB

PL 04537/0003

POM

*Anti-nerve agent medication given to Coalition forces in order to counteract the effects of an expected chemical weapons attack*

*French Foreign Legion soldiers wearing chemical warfare equipment, while preparing for the ground operations*

# AFTERMATH

## The immense damage wrought by the war lasted for generations, with lives, cultural heritage, economies and ecosystems destroyed

WORDS: TIM WILLIAMSON

Seven months of occupation had taken a horrific toll on Kuwait. 300,000 of its population had been made refugees, with over a thousand killed, and many more tortured or taken hostage.

Early in the occupation, the Kuwait National Museum and its museum of Islamic art was closed by the Iraqi army, and subsequently thousands of artefacts, books and archaeological objects were loaded onto trucks and taken to Baghdad. Many were painstakingly identified and returned to Kuwait in the months after liberation, while others were irrecoverable. As a parting gift, the retreating Iraqi army looted and burned homes, businesses and government buildings, while also seizing hostages. Not even the national zoo escaped from the destruction – while a number of exotic birds were stolen by the Iraqis, most of the zoo's remaining residents were killed and eaten by hungry soldiers.

The Kuwait Institute for Scientific Research did not escape either – decades of research was either stolen or lost in the destruction of the $18-million facility. Most controversially, over 700 of Kuwait's oil wells were set ablaze or sabotaged by the retreating occupiers, wreaking immeasurable damage as well as unleashing an environmental catastrophe.

Every day millions of barrels of oil spilled into the desert, out to sea or burned up into the atmosphere. It took thousands of fire crews up to nine months to quell the infernos, and cap the oil wells. Many fire fighters, Kuwaiti citizens and Coalition forces subsequently suffered from severe lung damage from the toxic clouds that spread over 800 miles. Decades later, many of the worst areas of the fires remain polluted by the blazes. Back in Iraq, the Saddam regime may have survived while its own army was all but destroyed by the Coalition, but it immediately faced a new threat at home. Seizing upon the perceived

weakness of the dictatorship, Iraqi opposition groups across the country attacked regime headquarters and Saddam's security services. Soon major cities and then whole provinces in southern and north-west Iraq fell to the rebels, many of whom were also deserting soldiers. However, expected support from the US – which had earlier encouraged a coup against Saddam – did not arrive. Instead, the rump of Saddam's loyal Republican Guard was able to pick off rebel strongholds systematically with superior firepower, tanks and helicopter gunships. Tens of thousands were killed as the regime brutally regained control, with the Shi'a and Kurdish minorities in particular targeted and punished. It would take until the Iraq War of 2003-2011, prosecuted in the wake of the September 11 attacks in the US and based on the rationale that Iraq had access to weapons of mass destruction and would use them to support al-Qaeda, for Saddam's regime to finally be toppled.

## "EVERY DAY MILLIONS OF BARRELS OF OIL SPILLED INTO THE DESERT, OUT TO SEA, OR BURNED UP"

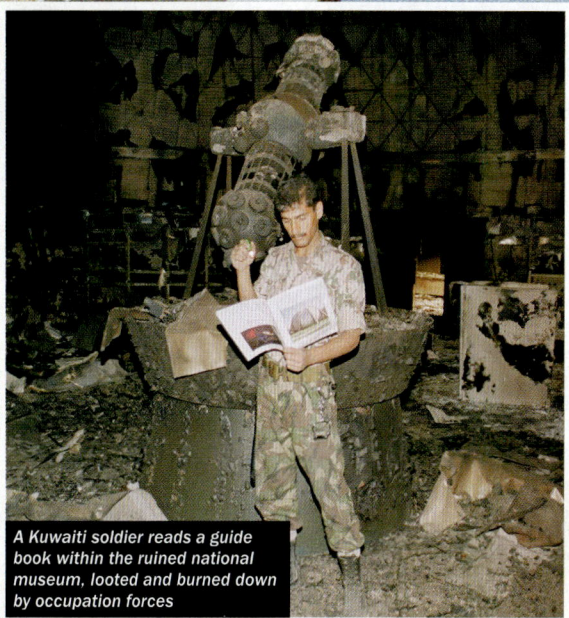

A Kuwaiti soldier reads a guide book within the ruined national museum, looted and burned down by occupation forces

# THE GULF WAR

## The facts and figures of Operation Desert Storm

## 697,000
▲ Troops served on active duty in the Gulf War for the United States of America

## $26 billion
▲ Amount lent to Iraq in aid by Saudi Arabia during its previous war with Iran

## 88,500
Tons of bombs dropped by the coalition in over 100,000 sorties

## 75
◄ Aircraft were lost by the coalition. Only 44 of these were a result of Iraqi defence measures

## 39
◄ Countries participated in the coalition of forces against Iraq

▼ Length of the war from invasion to liberation

## 6 months
## 3 weeks
## 5 days

## 206,861
▲ US veterans have claimed benefits for injuries and illness from combat in the Gulf War

## $61 billion
▲ Cost of the Gulf War to the USA. The cost to the American taxpayer was $7 billion, working out at $26.92 per American citizen

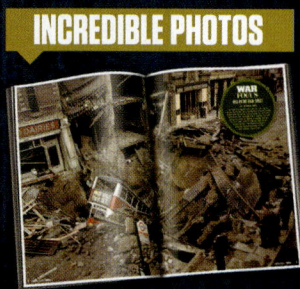